D0744499

Origins of Japanese Wealth and Power

Origins of Japanese Wealth and Power

Reconciling Confucianism and Capitalism, 1830–1885

John H. Sagers

ORIGINS OF JAPANESE WEALTH AND POWER
© John H. Sagers, 2006.

First published in 2006 by
PALGRAVE MACMILLAN™
175 Fifth Avenue, New York, N.Y. 10010 and
Houndmills, Basingstoke, Hampshire, England RG21 6XS
Companies and representatives throughout the world.

PALGRAVE MACMILLAN is the global academic imprint of the Palgrave Macmillan division of St. Martin's Press, LLC and of Palgrave Macmillan Ltd. Macmillan® is a registered trademark in the United States, United Kingdom and other countries. Palgrave is a registered trademark in the European Union and other countries.

ISBN 1–4039–7111–0

Library of Congress Cataloging-in-Publication Data

Sagers, John H.
    Origins of Japanese wealth and power : reconciling Confucianism and capitalism, 1830–1885 / John H. Sagers.
        p. cm.
    Includes bibliographical references and index.
    ISBN 1–4039–7111–0
    1. Japan—Economic conditions—19th century. 2. Japan—Economic policy—19th century. 3. Capitalism—Japan—Religious aspects—Confucianism—History—19th century. I. Title.
HC462.6.S234 2005
338.952′009′034—dc22   2005046296

A catalogue record for this book is available from the British Library.

Design by Newgen Imaging Systems (P) Ltd., Chennai, India.

First edition: January 2006

10 9 8 7 6 5 4 3 2 1

Printed in the United States of America.

For scholars, past, present, and future

Contents

List of Illustrations

Figures

Table

Acknowledgments

I would like to thank Kenneth Pyle, Kozo Yamamura, James Palais, and Kent Guy whose sage wisdom guided this project as a dissertation at the University of Washington. In Japan, I am indebted to Igarashi Akio, Matsumoto Sannosuke, Mark Caprio, and the faculty and staff of Rikkyo University in Tokyo for their guidance and support. Thanks also to Steven Ericson, Katalin Ferber, Susan Hanley, Chalmers Johnson, Mark Metzler, Luke Roberts, my colleagues at Linfield College, and two anonymous reviewers for helpful comments and encouragement, and to Anthony Wahl and the staff at Palgrave Macmillan who expertly shepherded this project to completion.

I am also most grateful for generous financial support from the Japan-US Education Commission's Fulbright Fellowship, the U.S. Department of Education's Foreign Language and Area Studies Fellowship, a Henry M. Jackson School of International Studies Fellowship, a Sanwa Bank Dissertation Grant, and a Linfield College Student-Faculty Collaborative Research Grant.

Finally, my profound appreciation goes to parents Bob and Ann Sagers, parents-in-law Jim and Bonnie Churchwell, wife Wendy, and sons Robert and Thomas for their love, faith, and patience.

Notes on the Text

Japanese and Chinese names have been rendered according to East Asian convention with the family name first, except in instances when an author writing in English uses a different order. The Hepburn system has been used for the Romanization for Japanese and pinyin for Chinese words. Macrons have been used to denote long Japanese vowels, except for well-known terms and places such as shogun and Tokyo. Original characters for important names and terms appear in the glossary.

Introduction

In 1868, a group of samurai from the domains of Satsuma and Chōshū overthrew the Tokugawa shogun and proclaimed the restoration of the Emperor Meiji as the head of state. The top priority of the new government was the revision of the humiliating treaties that the shogun had negotiated with the Western powers. To accomplish this and to restore their country's independence, Japanese government leaders believed that it was imperative for Japan to build its economic and military power.

Facing potential Western colonization, the desire for wealth and power was certainly understandable, but what was it that philosophically prepared early Meiji Japanese government leaders to accept capitalist institutions of economic organization? Clearly, Japan's radical institutional reforms of the 1870s and early 1880s depended on a dramatic shift in political and economic philosophy that was unusual in world history. As historian Thomas Smith once observed, "Communities in danger do not necessarily seek safety in innovation; commonly they reaffirm tradition and cling to it more resolutely."[1] Somehow, these Japanese government leaders departed from their Confucian samurai intellectual heritages (eschewing the pursuit of private gain as morally reprehensible) and embraced industrial capitalism. This book is about the evolution of economic thought in the last decades of the Tokugawa period that prepared Japanese government leaders after 1868 to conceive of market activity as a force that, with proper management, could benefit the national state.

Since the 1982 publication of Chalmers Johnson's *MITI and the Japanese Miracle*, interest in Japanese industrial policy and developmental institutions has grown dramatically.[2] Given a desire to explain the current state of Japan's economic system, it is understandable that many social scientists have focused their attention on more recent history. Their analyses of the Japanese government's response to the crises of The Great Depression and World War II have greatly advanced our knowledge of Japan's institutional development in the twentieth century.

Between 1925 and 1945, government officials became much more powerful in economic affairs than in previous eras. With bureaucratic leadership, mechanisms such as preferential government financing, state sponsored cartels, and centralized economic planning became important means of promoting industries considered necessary to support Japan's war effort. Bai Gao's 1997 book explores the role of economic ideology in policy making from the 1930s but includes only a brief discussion of earlier developments.[3] Noguchi Yukio's *Senkyūhyakuyonjūnen taisei* (The 1940 System) has gone as far as to say that Japanese capitalism's distinctive characteristics did not exist before the crises of the Great Depression and World War II.[4]

However, these scholars miss an important part of the story by beginning their study with the mid-1920s. Others have suggested that Japanese developmental thought can be traced to a much earlier period. Richard Samuels' study of the connection between military and civilian technology in the wartime and postwar periods mentions, in passing, that the government's role in technological development had its roots early in the modern era.[5] William Wray, in his book on the development of the Japanese shipping industry, points out that the government was subsidizing this key industry as early as the 1870s.[6]

Although historians have understood the importance of the Meiji period to the later evolution of the developmental state, there has been surprisingly little analysis and discussion of the role of economic thought in the government's industrial policy. There are several reasons for this gap in our understanding. First, the problem falls between disciplinary boundaries. Economic historians have tended to focus their attention on the role of economic aggregates such as capital accumulation, labor supply, and technology transfer. Their treatment of government policy focuses on what happened and how it affected the economy without analyzing the thought behind the policies. Conversely, intellectual historians have concentrated their attention on the rise of Japanese political nationalism and national consciousness.

Nakamura Takafusa's *Economic Growth in Prewar Japan*, for example, discusses in detail the changes in economic aggregates such as capital accumulation, labor supply, money supply, and technology levels. Nakamura assigns an important role of initiating Japan's economic development to state leadership, but he takes the goal of industrialization itself for granted. He writes, "This was the world of power politics. As a neophyte modern state, Japan had no choice but to resist the great powers, as expressed in the popular Meiji era slogan *fukoku kyōhei*, 'a rich country and a strong army.' "[7]

Henry Rosovsky labels the years between 1868 and 1885 as a crucial "transition period" when the Meiji government laid the institutional foundation to reach its economic development goals. Defending his approach against economists who tend to downplay the importance of government policy in industrial development, Rosovsky argues, "Primary focus on government activity during transition can be justified. Comparative economic history tells us that countries beginning industrialization in a setting of relative backwardness require leadership and strong action to get started. More or less spontaneous modern economic growth may have been the case in Great Britain, but it is difficult to find elsewhere."[8] The transition period was one of crisis in Japanese history when ideas of how to remake Japan as a modern power had profound import.

Sydney Crawcour adds to Rosovsky's notion of the transition period by outlining the Tokugawa era trends that contributed to Japanese policy makers' ability to realize modern economic growth. Crawcour writes, "Although there is much to be said for the view that Restoration leaders adopted the objective of industrial capitalism because they judged this to be the source of Western power, ideas of economic growth as a solution to financial problems had been current for a century before the Restoration."[9]

In his pioneering (1955) book on early Meiji industrial policy, Thomas Smith also outlines the debt that the Meiji leaders owed to Tokugawa precedent.

> In the development of modern industry the Tokugawa and *han* governments anticipated several important features of the industrial policy of the Meiji government. Government ownership and management of industry were salient features of the early Meiji period and were partly the result of the new government's inheriting the enterprises developed by its predecessors; in extending the principle to new fields of industry, the Meiji government was following Tokugawa example. In the operation of these enterprises, the Meiji government made use of foreign engineers and technicians, a policy already laid down in the Tokugawa period; and it was likewise following precedent in supporting training programs both in Japan and abroad to provide qualified personnel who would take over technical and managerial positions from foreigners.[10]

Although he implies a connection between Tokugawa economic ideas and Meiji policy, Smith leaves unanswered the question of how the Meiji oligarchs drew from their experience as domain officials and integrated this experience with Western ideas of political economy.

In his work on Dazai Shundai, Honda Toshiaki, and other scholars in the Confucian tradition, Testuo Najita has shown that modern Japanese ideas of the state's proper relationship to economic activity grew out of the late-eighteenth- and early-nineteenth-century political economy discourse. Najita argues that this discourse created a "conceptual consciousness" through which Meiji Japanese interpreted the problems they faced, but he does not elaborate on how this affected the Japanese government policy. Instead he leaves us with a challenge, "It does not take much looking to find the mercantilist thinking outlined by Honda in all of the major political leaders of the Ishin."[11]

In Japanese language historiography, a whole subfield of intellectual history has been devoted to economic thought. Honjō Eijirō pioneered the field in the 1930s and 1940s with biographical portraits of leading intellectual figures in the development of Japanese economics. These portraits traced the evolution of economic thought from Tokugawa Confucian scholars who addressed economic issues to the import of Western economic theory in the late nineteenth and early twentieth centuries. In the 1950s and 1960s, scholars such as Sumiya Etsuji and Tsukatani Akihiro followed Honjō's lead in writing comprehensive histories of Japanese economic thought emphasizing the lines of continuity between the late Tokugawa and early Meiji periods.[12]

In 1969, Chō Yukio and Sumiya Kazuhiko edited a two-volume study on modern economic thought that examined the evolution of Japanese economic ideology in government policy circles. This work included chapters on the debates between liberalism and the government's industrial promotion campaigns, nationalism, and the rural industry movement in the 1870s, and the debates between liberals and the German Historical School in the 1890s. More recently, Sugihara Shirō and others have compiled a survey of Japanese economic thought entitled *Japan's Nihon no keizai shisōshi no yonhyakunen* (Four Hundred Years of Economic Thought).[13] This work includes excerpts of major economists from the debates on political economy in the late seventeenth century to economic planning during the 1960s high growth era. These works underscore the importance of treating economics as a historically evolving set of ideas rather than as natural principles.

Fujita Teiichirō studied the Wakayama domain and showed that the domain officials enacted a set of policies that closely resembled European mercantilism. Fujita labeled this indigenous Japanese mercantilism as "*kokueki* thought" because officials justified their policies with the term *kokueki*, which can be translated as the country's interest, profit, or advantage and which appeared in Japanese in the seventeenth century without a known precedent in classical Chinese.

According to Fujita, the essence of *kokueki* thought was the "doctrine of supplying one's own needs through one's own production" or self-sufficiency. The thought also stressed the accumulation of precious metals rather than agricultural production as the root of wealth. In this, economic nationalism was a departure from the Confucian agrarian view of the economy toward a greater emphasis on commerce.

Consequently, it became morally acceptable for domains and nations to pursue their commercial interests, but the individual pursuit of profit was perceived negatively in Japanese ideology throughout the Meiji period. Byron Marshall's study of Meiji business ideology shows that modern business entrepreneurship was rationalized in terms of service to the nation rather than private gain. Business leaders such as Iwasaki Yatarō, who founded the Mitsubishi company, saw themselves not as greedy merchants, but rather as the heirs of the *shishi* who carried out a new kind of war with the foreigners through trade.[14] In a similar vein, Fujita wrote, "Can we not say that '*kokueki*' was the spirit of Japanese capitalism, at least in its Meiji form? . . . It was because of this that samurai even at daimyo level overcame the notion of commerce as vulgar and engaged in business enterprise."[15]

Luke Roberts in his recent study of the rise of economic nationalism in Tosa argues that mercantilist thinking arose first among the merchants and was later appropriated by the samurai officials. In Roberts's view, economic nationalism " 'decentered' the lord and 'centered' the country in political economic thought and thereby began changing the relationship between government and its people."[16] This insight is important because it shows that the concept of *kokueki* allowed merchants and peasants to think in terms of profit to the domain rather than simply to their lord. It was then possible to conceive of a commonwealth in which personal profit and community profit could be achieved simultaneously. Where Roberts emphasizes the merchants carving out a space for more mercantile activity, we can also see the domain bureaucrats trying to harness the profit motive of the merchants for state goals. In a sense, both mercantile and state interests overlapped as domains resorted to commercial promotion to solve their financial distress.

To illustrate the evolution of economic ideas across the Meiji Restoration, this book focuses on the domain of Satsuma, the home of several key economic policy makers in the Meiji government. In 1800, Satsuma was at the periphery of the Japanese economy. It had several export commodities including rice, sugar, and processed fish. Yet, the domain could not solve its chronic trade deficits with the Tokugawa Shogunate-dominated market centers in Kyoto, Osaka, and Edo. Many other domains were in a similarly dismal financial state by the second half of the Tokugawa period. Sensing this problem, entrepreneurial thinkers proposed the unorthodox solution that domains pay more attention to exploiting commercial opportunities. This went against the grain of the Confucian view of merchants as the lowest form of humanity and commerce as beneath the dignity of government. To reconcile this, rulers justified their concern with economic affairs as part of their duty to extend benevolence to the people, which required sufficient revenue. Soon daimyo were supporting anything that contributed to the domain's treasury.

In Satsuma, the daimyo invited a management consultant to give economic development advice in the late 1820s. The advice was rather simple and straightforward: look for some products that are selling well in the Japanese nationwide market and learn to make them. This would cut dependence on imports and, eventually, lead to profitable exports. Both would have a positive effect on the domain's treasury. To accomplish this, the domain should dispatch some bright people to the region that produced the best of a given good. Once these pioneers learned the necessary skills, they could teach them to others.

Satsuma implemented this simple plan and within twenty years accumulated an enviable surplus of wealth. In the 1840s, Western ships approached the Ryūkyū Islands seeking a trade treaty. As the suzerain of the island kingdom, the Satsuma daimyo had to find a solution to the crisis. Commodore Matthew Perry's 1853 American naval mission that ultimately forced the shogun to open Japan to limited trade is usually remembered as the beginning of the Tokugawa's foreign crisis. It is interesting to note that the Satsuma daimyo encountered similar problems nearly a decade earlier and quickly began a self-strengthening campaign. Using Western books and studying samples, Satsuma officials rapidly learned to make ships, steel furnaces, and cannon.

In this atmosphere, several future leaders of Meiji economic development including Godai Tomoatsu, Ōkubo Toshimichi, Kuroda Kiyotaka, Matsukata Masayoshi, and Maeda Masana came of age as samurai officials. They greatly admired their progressive lord Shimazu Nariakira, who spurred Satsuma to develop modern technology and the export industries to pay for it. By the time of the Restoration, an understanding of economic growth as the foundation for state power had become second nature.

Under Ōkubo in the 1870s, the Meiji government began to establish the basic institutions of capitalism including property rights for land and modern banking and currency systems.[17] To assist private entrepreneurs competing with Western industries, the government also launched several model factories to teach the Japanese the latest in mining, textile, and steel technology. These industrial projects were expensive, and in 1881, Matsukata Masayoshi, as the newly appointed Finance Minister, presided over their sale to private parties as a part of a general policy of fiscal retrenchment.

In his 1884 *Kōgyō iken* ("Opinion on the Encouragement of Enterprise"), Maeda Masana, a high ranking official in the Ministry of Agriculture and Commerce and former Satsuma samurai, criticized Matsukata's cutbacks for the hardship they inflicted on small business. He called for renewed government support of rural enterprises. His *Kōgyō iken* report showed that even in the new capitalist environment, officials retained a sense of moral obligation to protect the people's welfare.

The story of how officials from a highly peripheral "late developing" domain made their way to the very center of modern Japanese economic development policy helps us better understand the continuities of thought across the Meiji Restoration. Previous experience with economic difficulties in the Tokugawa system prepared early Meiji leaders to understand and respond the challenges Japan faced integrating into international markets. Ultimately, realism required them to accept capitalist principles of economic organization, but the Confucian notion that government officials had a duty to guide economic activity for higher moral ends remained strong.

CHAPTER 1

Confucian Statecraft and Ideological Innovation

The Tokugawa era (1600–1868) was crucial to the evolution of the economic ideology, which prepared the leaders of modern Japan to accept capitalism in the late nineteenth century. During this 250 years of peace, commerce flourished and state officials in feudal domains increasingly looked for ways to exploit this commercial growth to solve their own chronic financial problems. To take advantage of the new opportunities afforded by the changing economic environment, earlier notions of commerce as a dirty business beneath the dignity of the cultured elite had to be modified.

The philosophical changes that took place were not entirely cynical or pragmatic. Many Japanese scholars and officials schooled in the Confucian tradition seemed to be genuinely concerned with finding ways to reconcile new commercial policies with strongly held moral principles. Rather than overturning their beliefs entirely, they searched for alternative precedents in classical literature. Understanding the maintenance of order as an essential prerequisite to a state's ability to promote moral conduct, intellectuals took a fresh look at the powerful rulers who had established strong states in Chinese and Japanese history. What they found was that wealth and power were the key tools with which order could be maintained and moral virtue promoted.

Confucianism was the central philosophy of the domain schools in which young samurai were educated and which formed the foundation of the educated elite's worldview during the Tokugawa period. To understand where the Meiji leaders' economic ideas originated, we must first explore the changes occurring in Confucian thought in the late seventeenth century in response to commercialization.

During the Tokugawa era, commercial growth caused the gap to widen between the orthodox Confucian ideal of a stable society and the reality of the ruling class' financial distress. With their income in terms of rice and their expenses in cash, feudal lords (daimyo) and their samurai retainers suffered from the declining value of rice relative to other goods. While Confucian conservatives tried to reverse the effects of commercialization with sumptuary edicts, reformers began to justify the ruling class' engagement in commerce. These reformers may have been more flexible, but they were by no means revolutionary and carefully put their policy proposals in terms of classical precedent. By the late eighteenth century, a new vision of the ruler's relationship to economic activity emerged that put commercial gain in service of the state's moral ends. The urgency with which the daimyo pursued commercial advantage intensified as they competed with one another for profits in trade within the whole Japanese market. To justify this shift in economic policies, some thinkers tried to reconcile commerce with Confucian moral ideas. These philosophers discussed trade not in its own right but in terms of the ruler's moral obligation to "order the realm and save the people" (*keisei saimin*) and to promote the domain states' "national interest" (*kokueki*). A contraction of the characters for *keisei saimin* was used to translate the term economics in to modern Japanese as *keizai*. During the Tokugawa period the term for country *koku* was used for the feudal domains. Later it came to mean all of Japan. The term *eki* seems to have encompassed both political "interests" and economic "profit."

As economic change forced ruling officials to reevaluate how they financed their governments, philosophical innovators proposed new ways of viewing commercial activity. Rather than suppressing commerce for its negative effect on public morals as traditional Confucians had done, the proponents of *keisei saimin* and *kokueki* thought embraced commerce as the means through which rulers could enhance their moral capacity. This was an important ideological shift because it meant that domain state leaders increasingly saw trade as vital to their strategic interests relative to one another and crucial to the survival of their realms.

Confucian Philosophy and Tokugawa Legitimacy

Any discussion of a modern Japanese strategic vision for economic development must begin with the Tokugawa regime. For over two and a half centuries, Japan was ordered according to the institutions and ideology that the Tokugawa established and propagated. This institutional matrix profoundly shaped how economic issues were defined, debated, and resolved. Tokugawa Confucian ideology provided the philosophical foundation for an evolving understanding of economic activity.

The driving concern of the Tokugawa rulers was order. After a century of civil war between feudal states, Oda Nobunaga began the process of unification by subduing rival feudal lords. Toyotomi Hideyoshi continued this work, and by the time of his death in 1598, he had succeeded in uniting Japan. After Hideyoshi's death, two coalitions of daimyo emerged. Tokugawa Ieyasu led one coalition formed mainly of daimyo from eastern Japan. Their opponents were mostly comprised of daimyo from west of Osaka. In 1600, the Tokugawa forces won a decisive victory at Sekigahara in the mountains near Kyoto and forced their opponents to capitulate to Ieyasu's rule. Three years later, the emperor granted Tokugawa Ieyasu the title of "shogun" and formally delegated the authority to rule Japan. With the final fall of Osaka castle and the extermination of the Toyotomi line in 1615, Tokugawa rule was secure. Still fearing that rival lords would challenge their hegemony, the Tokugawa carefully constructed a regime to maintain order.

From the perspective of economic thought, it is interesting to note that land in the Tokugawa system was apportioned not by area but rather by productive capacity. The *koku* (4.96 bushels) was a unit of grain that roughly corresponded to the amount of rice needed to feed one person for one year. In their struggle for survival with one another, the daimyo had come to realize that their success or failure hinged on their land's output and the wealth that it generated. In the 1580s, Hideyoshi had ordered cadastral surveys of all village lands in Japan and used the assessment of their productive capacity in *koku* to assign daimyo lands. A daimyo's power and prestige was directly related to the assessed value of his lands.[1]

The Tokugawa continued Oda Nobunaga's and Toyotomi Hideyoshi's earlier practices of confiscating land from defeated rivals and using it to reward loyal supporters. Tokugawa Ieyasu also maintained Hideyoshi's classification of daimyo in terms of their relationship to his own household. The Tokugawa house itself controlled 6.8 million *koku*. Houses related to the Tokugawa (*shimpan*) owned 2.6 million *koku*. "House daimyo" (*fudai*) allied with the Tokugawa at the time of Sekigahara controlled 6.7 million *koku*. And the "outer lords" (*tozama*), who had risen independently during the Warring States period to become formidable powers in their own rights, controlled 9.8 million *koku*. With Tokugawa relatives and allies controlling over 60 percent of the total, the shogunate was in a hegemonic, albeit not omnipotent, position.[2]

As traditional enemies of the Tokugawa still controlled nearly half of the resources in Japan, early shogunate leaders had to carefully construct a system of institutional controls. The alternate attendance system was one of the most important of these controls. It required each daimyo to spend every other year in Edo serving the shogun. When the daimyo returned to his home domain, his wife and heir were left in Edo as hostages. The system was effective in maintaining surveillance over the daimyo.

To bring order to the society, the Tokugawa continued Hideyoshi's policy of freezing the social class structure by limiting mobility between warrior, peasant, artisan, and merchant classes. Where many peasant farmers had taken up arms and served their lords in times of trouble, the distinction between the warrior aristocracy and commoners was more sharply drawn. After Hideyoshi's famous "sword hunt," only samurai could bear arms and the two swords became a badge of their status. Even within the ruling warrior class, a hierarchy of ranks gradually solidified and it became more difficult for lower ranking samurai to secure promotion. The freezing of the hierarchical system of social ranks helped stabilize the Tokugawa order.

Confucianism provided Tokugawa intellectuals with a long philosophical tradition from which to draw ordering principles. The Chinese philosopher Kong Fuzi (551–479 BC) is generally known in the West by the Latinized name Confucius. Confucius lived at a time of near constant warfare between competing principalities. So, it is not surprising that his philosophy would place a high value on benevolence, obedience, and decorum. Confucius idealized the Duke of Zhou as a strong leader who led by moral example and presided over a realm characterized by benevolence and filial piety. Conversely, Confucius and his disciples believed that ambition, competition, and the pursuit of profit were divisive and harmful to social order. As Confucius said, "The gentleman understands what is moral. The small man understands what is profitable."[3] For Confucius, social harmony and peace could be achieved only if people put aside their petty ambitions and cultivated themselves through attention to the duties to which heaven had entrusted them.

Later scholars in the Confucian tradition elaborated on this idea. When the philosopher Mencius (Mengzi, 372–286 BC) had an audience with King Hui of Liang, the king asked, "You have come all this distance, thinking nothing of a thousand *li*. You must surely have some way of profiting my state?" To this, Mencius responded,

> Your Majesty, what is the point of mentioning the word "profit"? All that matters is that there should be benevolence and rightness. If Your Majesty says, "How can I profit my state?" and the Counselors say, "How can I

profit my family?" and the Gentlemen and Commoners say, "How can I profit my person?" then those above and those below will be trying to profit at the expense of one another and the state will be imperiled. When regicide is committed in a state of ten thousand chariots, it is certain to be committed in a state of a thousand chariots and when it is committed in a state with a thousand chariots, it is certain to be by a vassal with a hundred chariots. A share of a thousand in ten thousand or a hundred in a thousand is by no means insignificant, yet if profit is put before rightness, there is no satisfaction short of total usurpation. No benevolent man ever abandons his parents, and no dutiful man ever puts his prince last. Perhaps you will now endorse what I have said, "All that matters is that there should be benevolence and rightness. What is the point of mentioning the word 'profit'?"[4]

In feudal regimes, competition was often equated with treachery and the pursuit of gain almost always came at someone else's expense.[5] Although Mencius was addressing the issue of political rivalries and the potential for treason among vassals, a similar hostility toward self-interested gain applied to commerce. Here we see that Confucian philosophers had a long tradition of animosity toward the idea of profit and toward the pursuit of narrow self-interest. Another often cited example of this sentiment is the debate recorded in 81 BC between Confucian scholars and government ministers of the Han Dynasty. Government officials pragmatically argued that a state monopoly of key commodities was crucial to financing military campaigns against the Xiongnu people on the northern frontier. To this, Confucian philosophers protested,

> We have heard that the way to rule lies in preventing frivolity while encouraging morality, in suppressing the pursuit of profit while opening the way for benevolence and duty. When profit is not emphasized, civilization flourishes and the customs of the people improve.
>
> Recently, a system of salt and iron monopolies, a liquor excise tax, and an equable marketing system have been established throughout the country. These represent financial competition with the people which undermines their native honesty and promotes selfishness. As a result, few among the people take up fundamental pursuits [agriculture] while many flock to the secondary [trade and industry]. When artificiality thrives, simplicity declines; when the secondary flourishes, the basic decays. Stress on the secondary makes people decadent; emphasis on the basic keeps them unsophisticated. When the people are unsophisticated, wealth abounds; when they are extravagant, cold and hunger ensue.[6]

State ministers argued that the state monopolies would protect the people both by providing funds from military defense and by keeping these businesses out of the hands of greedy merchants. The Confucians, however, believed that a well-ordered state was based fundamentally on agriculture and that manufacturing and trade only led to avarice that would draw people away from their primary occupations.

During the Chinese Song Dynasty, Zhu Xi (1130–1200) and other philosophers contributed to a "Neo-Confucian" revival as they provided an important synthesis of Confucian ideals of enduring moral norms and the Taoist and Buddhist sense that all reality was inherently impermanent and unstable. The Mongol Yuan Dynasty institutionalized Zhu Xi's commentaries as the orthodox interpretation of the Confucian classics including *Analects, Mencius, Doctrine of the Mean*, and the *Great Learning* by making them required reading for the civil service examination in 1313. Zhu Xi's basic theory was that natural principle (*li*) could be discerned rationally through study of the classics. This idea served the political authorities by legitimating the present regime as the "Way" of heaven or nature.[7]

Zhu Xi's distinction between the enduring patterns in history, which he called *li*, and the ephemeral manifestations of these patterns, which he called *qi*, had a variety of implications and could be deployed in different ways depending upon one's political perspective. Intellectuals and bureaucrats seeking to preserve the status quo emphasized *li* side of Zhu Xi's metaphysical formulation. The current political order was simply the product of heaven's principles and should not be altered. Opponents proposing heterodox policies, on the other hand, argued that much that was understood as enduring *li* may actually be the ephemeral *qi* of a certain age that was destined to change with the times.

At the beginning of the Tokugawa period, Zhu Xi's understanding of Confucianism with its emphasis on social harmony and order was well suited for Japanese purposes. Although Tokugawa Ieyasu studied Chinese classical literature well before he established the bakufu, as intellectual historian Masao Maruyama concluded, "[he] was interested in Confucianism because of its fundamental moral principles and its concepts of political legitimacy, not because of its literary or exegetic values."[8] Confucianism gradually transformed the warrior aristocracy into a class of scholar-officials who were also expected to maintain military proficiency and discipline. Confucian philosophy stressed that everyone in a society should know their places and perform the duties that Heaven had entrusted to them. The ruler was to rule with wisdom and benevolence and the subject was to serve with diligence. Hayashi Razan (1583–1657), Tokugawa Ieyasu's Confucian advisor, defined the "Way" as follows: "Their [the Sages'] Way consists of nothing else than the moral obligations between sovereign and subject, father and child, husband and wife, elder and younger brother, and friend and friend."[9]

Hayashi demonstrated several important elements of Tokugawa Confucian orthodox ideology. A set of natural principles formed the basis of human virtue. These principles could be ascertained by studying the behavior of the sage kings in the classics. The moral way that became apparent from this study was defined as proper behavior within one's social relationships, submission to superiors, benevolence to inferiors, and the like. With the exception of friend and friend, each of the Confucian relationships was hierarchical. People had duties rather than rights and Confucianism emphasized the moral obligation of individuals to sacrifice for the good of the state.

This discussion of Confucianism is important in the study of economic ideology because it establishes a fundamental assumption that would distinguish the Japanese state's view of economics from later liberal economic theory: *the fruit of an individual's labor belongs first and foremost to the state.* Whatever portion the individual was allowed to keep was thanks to the sovereign's benevolence rather than any inherent individual rights.

This view was clear in the Tokugawa economy. The Confucian ideal was based on peasants engaged in subsistence agriculture. The ruler would take any surplus in the form of grain taxes. The system would then theoretically maintain a state of static equilibrium. After the chaos of the Warring States era of the fifteenth and sixteenth centuries when Japanese regional warlords were able to ignore the Ashikaga shogunate's authority and make war on one another, this kind of stability must have been attractive.

Another important influence that Confucianism had on economic thought was a holistic approach to statecraft. This meant that there was no conceptual division between polity, economy, and society. All three served the interests of the feudal lord and helped him fulfill his moral obligation to govern his province with benevolence. Kumazawa Banzan (1619–1691) noted the connection between economic activity and the ruler's duty when he wrote, "Benevolent rule cannot be extended throughout the land without first developing our material wealth."[10]

For Kumazawa, wealth was not to be pursued for its own sake, but rather as a tool with which a ruler could alleviate the suffering of his subjects. Later in the same passage, he noted that the samurai class' economic hardship was a problem that destabilized the society. With *rōnin* (masterless samurai) becoming increasingly desperate, crime and violent protest became more likely. It was the ruler's responsibility to correct the problem and economic wealth was necessary to do that.

Like the Confucian scholars protesting the Han Dynasty's salt monopolies, Kumazawa believed that manufacturing and trade took people away from agriculture, which he understood to be the most important source of wealth. He even went so far as to advocate policies to arrest market growth including eliminating coins as media of exchange and establishing a barter economy based on grain to refocus the people's attention on agriculture:

> The treasure of the people is grain. Gold, silver, copper and so forth are the servants of grain. They come after grain . . . The enlightened ruler stores grain plentifully for the people, and, since all buying and selling is performed with grain, the people enjoy abundance . . . It is difficult to transport large quantities of grain, and therefore, if grain is used [as a means of exchange], trade cannot be easily monopolized. So the price of goods is lowered and luxury does not increase. Samurai and farmers are prosperous, while artisans and merchants also have secure fortunes.[11]

Several points in the Confucian view of economy and the conservative approach to reconciling the market to moral beliefs are apparent here. First, the people's economic well being was the ruler's responsibility. Second, the money economy was considered a subversive force that worked against the moral obligations of the state. Third, Confucians took the physiocratic view that agriculture was the wellspring of wealth and prosperity. Fourth, the pursuit of material luxury was bad for public morals and should be discouraged.

All these points fit together in a holistic view of the political economy. Economics could not be separated from the larger whole of human activity. Samurai officials believed that only government institutions, in keeping with Confucian moral principles, could promote true prosperity. This holistic approach would prove important in later discourse as economic policies were debated on their moral as well as practical merits.

Thus, it is important to begin our inquiry into Japanese economic thought and policy with Tokugawa Confucianism. Confucianism laid the conceptual groundwork for a philosophy of how the individual related to the national whole. It also placed economics in the larger context of statecraft. Where liberal economic theories, which Japanese leaders would later encounter, celebrated individual innovation and pursuit of profit as the motivating force for social progress, Confucianism had a very different understanding of social organization in which wise leaders built a moral order precisely by restraining individual passions.

Economic Growth and Responses to Ideological Anomaly

Tokugawa institutions and ideology were designed to maintain a status quo that had been painfully wrought in the turmoil of civil war. Over time, however, economic growth drastically altered relations between the social classes and challenged moral ideals. As farmers and merchants prospered, their superiors in the samurai class endured economic hardship. Over time, ideology and reality diverged and what to do about it became the subject of vigorous debate. The attempt to reconcile Confucian thought with new economic realities produced both conservative reaction and innovative lines of inquiry. The most important of these new ideas was the historicist view of ethical leadership.

Commercial activity blossomed when the civil wars of the Warring States period ended and it accelerated under the Tokugawa peace. Some historians have put the economic growth rate at 0.78 to 1.34 percent annually from 1550 to 1700.[12] Peasants began to produce more crops such as cotton, tea, hemp, mulberry, indigo, vegetables, and tobacco for the market. A money economy expanded to facilitate market transactions.

Policies the Tokugawa had implemented for political control also fueled demand for commercial products. The maintenance of large samurai garrisons in castle towns accelerated urbanization. Merchants and artisans gathered around the castles to service the needs of the samurai. Merchants also obtained goods produced in the countryside as cash crops or handicrafts and sold them to the samurai in towns and cities.

The alternate attendance system requiring daimyo to divide their time between their home domains and the shogun's capital perhaps had the most profound economic implications. Social life at Edo required the daimyo to maintain lavish mansions near the shogun's palace. The procession to and from Edo became an opportunity for the daimyo to display his wealth and splendor. In short, the daimyo's prestige and social standing were again reckoned in economic terms. In this way, the alternate attendance system placed a great financial burden on the daimyo. Kaga domain, for example, spent between one-third and one-half of its total revenue on its residence in Edo, retainers, and travel expenses.[13] This level of expenditure created great demand for a variety of products.

This expansion of commerce put pressure on the shogunate and domain treasuries. In addition to alternate attendance obligations, the shogun placed levies on the daimyo for infrastructure construction and repair. Rice tax revenues could not keep up with the growth of domain expenditures. As commercialization progressed in the seventeenth century, the general price level increased and the daimyo were forced to borrow from wealthy merchants to finance their revenue shortfalls.

Unfortunately, loans provided only short-term relief to the daimyo's financial distress. Rulers also resorted to debasing currency to ease their financial burden. The economic historian Miyamoto Matao has shown that inflation followed a cyclical pattern as the authorities debased currency and engaged in deficit financing to pay for their expenses, which in turn resulted in more money in circulation. This increase in the money supply contributed to a rise in effective demand, which drove prices up. When the shogun or the domains issued more debt or debased their coins, the cycle began again. Figure 1.1 shows how the change in the general price level fluctuated in the second half of the Tokugawa period in Kumamoto, near Satsuma on the island of Kyushu.

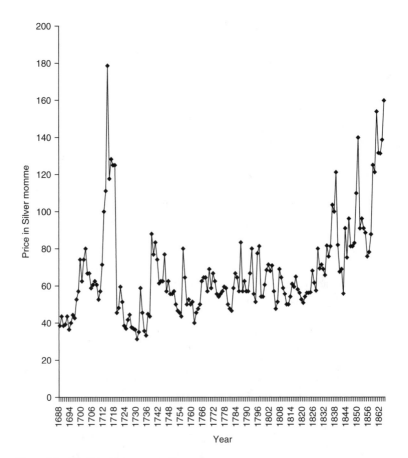

Figure 1.1 Rice Price Fluctuation in Kumamoto

Source: Iwahashi Masaru, *Kinsei Ninhon bukkashi no kenkyū* (Tokyo: Ōhara Shinseisha, 1981), 461–465.

As inflation caused daimyo cash expenditures to outrun their revenue collected in kind, domain financial administrators looked desperately for ways to cut costs. Since samurai stipends were one of the largest budget items, these were often sacrificed. Consequently, warriors who considered themselves the moral superiors of all others in society found themselves in debt to the lower classes.

These changes in prices had the effect of transferring income away from the warrior elite, who were dependent on agricultural taxes to the mercantile classes, who were actively engaged in commerce. This situation presented the Tokugawa ideological system with a serious anomaly. The greatest of feudal lords were becoming dependent upon the merchant class, which was theoretically at the bottom of the social hierarchy. This anomalous incongruence between wealth and social status posed a serious challenge to the Tokugawa Confucian orthodoxy.

Peasants were also becoming rich through the sale of cash crops and additional income derived from by-employments. These wealthy peasants (gōnō) engaged in a number of entrepreneurial activities including the production of paper, charcoal ink, pottery, lacquer ware, and woven cloth. These side occupations allowed farmers to use their time in the off-season to engage in productive activity. This increased productivity allowed the farmers' income to grow significantly and, as Susan Hanley has shown, their standard of living, in terms of material comfort and physical well being, was significantly enhanced.[14]

Farmers engaging in additional occupations to supplement their incomes accelerated the process of specialization and extension of market incentives from towns to the countryside.[15] Market incentives led many farmers to devote more of their time and energy to developing skills in businesses with a higher value added than the heavily taxed rice agriculture. Regional division of labor promoted efficiency, but observers often lamented the tendency of farmers to neglect farming to engage in more profitable commercial activities.[16]

With the distribution of wealth from market activity increasingly at odds with Confucian ideals of an agrarian, hierarchical, and harmonious social order, the need to reconcile ideals and reality was becoming apparent. Historian Thomas Kuhn's insights derived from the study of scientific revolutions are helpful in thinking about the process of ideological adjustment to new realities:

> Discovery commences with the awareness of anomaly, i.e., with the recognition that nature has somehow violated the paradigm-induced expectations that govern normal science. It then continues with a more or less extended exploration of the area of anomaly. And it closes only when the

paradigm theory has been adjusted so that the anomalous has become the expected.[17]

Typically, when confronting a discrepancy between theoretical beliefs and empirical observation, there are two choices: either reaffirm the theory and work to bring reality into line with beliefs or adjust the theory to more closely mirror observed phenomena. We might call these two approaches, "fundamentalist" and "realist".[18]

The Tokugawa elite's first response to the economic distress was understandably fundamentalist. Government officials blamed their problems on the people's moral failure rather than any inherent problem with Confucian principle. The obvious solution was to use moral exhortation to get more tax revenue out of the peasants and reduce samurai demand for consumer goods. The Kyōhō reforms (1716–1736) under Tokugawa Yoshimune had several fundamentalist tenets. First there was a strict frugality campaign continuing the tradition of sumptuary edicts. These regulations tried to curb daimyo and samurai spending. In 1718, Yoshimune issued instructions for the complete reminting of currency using both gold and silver coins. Yoshimune's officials also started the strict regulation of Edo moneychangers forcing them to cooperate with currency revaluation. In 1721, the shogunate regulated Edo merchants involved in the production and sale of luxury goods by organizing them into guilds. From 1722, Yoshimune called for renewed efforts in land reclamation to boost the shogunate's revenue. New tax regulations were established that ensured that a larger portion of agricultural production actually made it to the shogun's treasury. These measures had an initial degree of success with the shogunate increasing its average annual land tax revenue from 1.37 million *koku* to 1.52 million *koku* between 1716 and 1730. These gains, however, were made at the expense of the people and discontent mounted in the towns and villages.[19]

Despite attempts to return Japan to an earlier paradigm, the changes that had taken place in society could not be reversed. Gradually, some thinkers and policy makers realized that the fundamentalist approach could not meet the challenges of new social conditions. This did not mean, however, that they were ready to completely discard the Confucian philosophical system. Rather, they began to explore new ways to reconcile the reality of a commercial economy with Confucian philosophical principles.

In contrast to fundamentalists who hoped to roll back commercial development, realist reformers took commerce as given and looked for ways to adjust Confucian theory to match what they observed. During the latter half of the Tokugawa era, a wide range of thinkers conducted an extended exploration of the area of anomaly. This exploration is what subsequent historians have called a "discourse of political economy."[20] This discourse asked the basic question of how commercial development could be turned from the ruler's adversary into an ally to fulfill his moral obligation.

This ideological change was gradual and incremental. Realist reformers seeking to bring ideas in line with observed reality did not challenge the basic hierarchical social assumptions of Confucianism. Subjects still had a duty to serve with loyalty and devotion. Rulers still had a moral obligation to show benevolence to their subjects. The means with which rulers showed benevolence to their people, however, was an issue that generated considerable debate. In fact, this debate on how to obtain the material means to pursue benevolent ends provided an opening in Tokugawa Confucian thought for later ideological innovations.

To provide a framework for change, the realists adopted a historicist perspective on the nature of the Confucian Way. The Tokugawa ideologues argued that political, economic, and social institutions were based on timeless principle and that they should endure. The realists, however, adopted a historicist approach and argued that Tokugawa Ieyasu had displayed sage leadership not by implementing timeless principles, but rather by establishing an institutional order that was appropriate to a specific set of historical circumstances. Although moral goals remained consistent, the actual institutions used to reach these goals needed to be adjusted periodically.

The leading proponent of this historicist view was Ogyū Sorai (1666–1728). Sorai founded an action-oriented heterodox school that became known as "Ancient Learning" (*kogaku*) and sought to recapture the original spirit of the Chinese classical sages by rejecting later commentaries like Zhu Xi's. Sorai's father had been a physician to the shogun Tokugawa Tsunayoshi. After his early Confucian education, Sorai left Edo and dedicated himself to his personal scholarship.[21] In his writings, Sorai argued, contrary to Zhu Xi orthodoxy, that no one could ever know principles with any certainty. "The Way" was a fiction that rulers had devised to legitimate their policies. All human senses were subjective and unreliable so no one could say what constituted "the Way." The best that men could do was to study classical antiquity and try to recapture the social norms at the creation of the present order. For Sorai, this was the era of the sage kings in classical Chinese history. The sage was one who created the norms of society appropriate to the times without trying to legitimate them in principle.[22]

This was a crucial development for it cut political economy away from the moral authority of the Tokugawa Confucian orthodoxy.

Tokugawa Ieyasu, according to this new interpretation, had not founded a system based on timeless principles to be followed forevermore. Rather, he had acted wisely and decisively to establish an order appropriate to a given set of historical circumstances. It was then theoretically possible that the Tokugawa system might some day be inappropriate to the times and new sage leaders would emerge to create a new order. These developments had the effect of weakening the Tokugawa regime's monopoly on the "Way of Heaven" (*tendō*). The historicists acknowledged the reality of change and the need for different responses. If they could show that the current order did not constitute the end of natural principle, it logically followed that there was room for innovation to solve contemporary problems.

Although the connection between philosophical historicism and economic policy thinking may seem somewhat esoteric, it is of critical importance for understanding later Japanese approaches to economic development. It meant that policies would be judged not by their adherence to an abstract principle, but rather on their appropriateness to actual conditions. This notion of "appropriateness" would open the way for proper government to be tied to economic performance.

In sum, the Tokugawa peace, urbanization, and the alternate attendance system contributed to the rise of commercial activity in Japan. This commercial growth resulted in a dislocation between the Confucian ideal of a subsistence peasantry ruled by morally superior samurai and reality. The attempts of fundamentalist reformers to restrict commerce and extract more revenue from taxpayers was met with only moderate success. Eventually, realist thinkers began to probe the commercial question with an eye toward adjusting Confucian theory to take into consideration social reality. The point of departure for this inquiry was to question the Tokugawa monopoly of moral virtue. Historicists such as Ogyū Sorai saw "the Way" as a creative norm with which rulers devised policies and institutions appropriate to a given place in history. As historical circumstances changed, new sages would have to emerge to create appropriate institutions to carry out the ruler's moral obligation to act with benevolence toward his subjects. This provided an opportunity for aspiring sages to innovate new institutions for economic growth.

Commercial Solutions to Moral Problems

From the historicist's position that policy needed to be appropriate to historical conditions rather than abstract principles, thinkers called on the daimyo and shogun to recognize and exploit commercial opportunities and reject the physiocratic view of the economy based primarily on agriculture. Since these policy proposals were directly at odds with earlier disparagement of merchant activity, they had to be justified within the lexicon of Confucian political discourse. Intellectuals provided this justification with two key concepts. First, they argued that since it was the ruler's duty to "order the realm and save the people" (*keisei saimin*), every means available, including commerce, should be used to carry out this moral obligation. Second, if commerce was considered a tool with which a ruler showed compassion to the people, it was not much of a leap to say that the state's pursuit of profit was in the realm's interest (*kokueki*). In this way, thinkers and policy makers justified the state's pursuit of profit in trade in the context of Confucian morality.

Realist thinkers and officials admitted the reality of commerce and began to look for ways to use it to their domains' advantage. Sorai's disciple Dazai Shundai (1680–1747) elaborated on his master's teaching to provide the foundation for the ruler to improve his economic situation. Dazai had been a scholar in his own right studying in Kyoto and Osaka before entering Sorai's school later in life. His age and experience helped him to benefit from Sorai's teaching. As intellectual historian Tetsuo Najita has observed, "The quintessence of Ogyū's teachings, Dazai argued with greater clarity than the master himself, was for scholars to understand the creativity of the ancient kings in order that they might act in the present."[23]

Dazai was one of the first thinkers to openly advocate domain involvement in commercial affairs. Such activity had long been considered the realm of merchants and beneath the dignity of the warrior aristocracy. Dazai defined the terms of subsequent *keisei saimin* debates as follows,

> To rule the nation under heaven is called *keizai*. It is the concept of ordering the realm and saving the people. *Kei* refers to the threads that hold silk fabric together (the warp). It says in the *Book of Divination*, "The Gentleman is the thread holding the fabric together." In the *Doctrine of the Mean*, it says, "*Kei* is the great thread that binds together all under heaven." This thread is the governing thread. The cloth's length or warp is called *kei*. The width or weave is called *i*. When a craftswoman weaves silk fabric, she first sets up the warp threads. The parameters of those threads become the *kei*. Then the cloth is woven. *Kei* is the ordering principles.[24]

This showed a comprehensive view of political economy that included all elements of statecraft, which should be derived from studying the creative spirit of the ancient sages. "If he is to fulfill his duty and enrich the country and strengthen the military, the supreme ruler must not ever deviate from the Way of the Two Empires and Three Kingdoms."[25]

For Dazai, the important function of a ruler was to bring order to the realm. Consequently, he believed that the Legalists in the classical Chinese tradition had made a greater contribution to their civilization than later Confucian historians gave them credit:

> It is the sovereign's work to bring wealth to the country and strengthen the military, which is none other than the Way of the Two Empires and Three Kingdoms. At the end of the Zhou, various masters established the hundred schools of thought. In the Warring States that followed, it is said, Shen Buhai and Han Feizi became supreme by employing legalist punishments. It was not the way of the saints, but it was one side of ordering the realm and saving the people (keizai). Duke Xiao of Qin employed Shang Yang and strengthened the country. The First Emperor destroyed the six kingdoms and united all within the seas. He did not reinstate the various principalities, but made one country of all under heaven with administrative districts. Although the Qin died out after only three generations, the Han followed in the Qin's steps and the administrative system was used without change for almost two thousand years of history.[26]

For Dazai and other scholars of Ancient Studies, the Chinese Legalist tradition provided an important alternative to Confucian moralism. Although Confucian historians since the Han Dynasty had condemned the Qin emperors' ruthless ambition, Dazai argued that the Qin had created the institutional apparatus that brought order to China and put later dynasties in a position to show greater benevolence. Where Confucians typically emphasized leadership by moral example, Legalists contended that establishing institutions that harnessed natural human ambitions would better serve the ruler's ultimate objective of lasting peace and stability.[27]

Rather than relying on moral principles to address economic problems, Dazai advocated a realist approach to the problem. Using the metaphor of a physician ministering to a patient, he stressed the importance of immediate and appropriate action:

> In general, the technique of managing the economy is akin to a physician ministering to an illness. The fundamental approach to curing an ailment is to seek out its basic source, although in an emergency, the observable symptoms are directly treated. The same is true of the economy.[28]

According to Dazai, the economic problems of the domains needed to be addressed quickly with practical solutions. The metaphor of the economy as an organic entity similar to the human body was common in political economy discourse. The current financial distress of the daimyo and their samurai was a disease that could be cured. The economy was naturally healthy, but there was some pathology preventing its healthy operation. Dazai believed that the ruler could diagnose that problem and restore the economic functions of the body politic to proper health.

Dazai believed that the root of economic disease was in the government's failure to adjust to new commercial realities. He advocated the shogunate and domain governments take a more active approach to economic policy and engage in commercial activities. Some domains were already exploiting commercial opportunities and other daimyo could profit by their example:

> Like merchants, therefore, retainers on stipends and daimyo all tend to satisfy their needs with money and thus devise ways to acquire it. This may well be the most urgent task of the day. The best way to earn money is to trade. In one of the domains in the country, trade has been relied upon to meet expenses since ancient times. The daimyo of Tsushima governs a small domain, having rice yields of barely 20,000 *koku*. However, by buying commodities such as ginseng roots at an inexpensive rate from Korea, controlling these goods within the domain and selling them at high prices, he has more financial resources to spare than another daimyo with a rice income of 200,000 *koku*.[29]

Here Dazai was alerting daimyo to the dangers and opportunities that commerce afforded. To govern their domains effectively, daimyo had to acquire the necessary resources. Commercial interests in specialized products proved to be more lucrative than the traditional reliance on rice agriculture for revenue. The daimyo's involvement in commerce, then, was justified as the appropriate policy in his circumstances to generate the maximum resources with which to carry out his highest duty to "order the realm and save the people."

Dazai summed up his view as follows: "Those who would discuss *keizai* should know four things. First, they should know the times. Second, they should know the principles. Third, they should know conditions. Fourth, they should know human compassion."[30] From this we can see that to be effective, Dazai believed that traditional notions of moral principle and human compassion needed to be combined with a thorough knowledge of historical and geographic conditions.

Following the logic of ordering the realm and saving the people, trade became not only accepted within many Tokugawa domains, but was also seen as essential. As the daimyo tried to monopolize specialized products, they started to compete with one another for profit within Japan's national market. This competition further intensified the discourse on political economy. As daimyo competed with one another for wealth, power, and prestige within the Tokugawa system, chronic debt and trade deficits led domain officials to regard trade as a highly competitive enterprise in which one domain gained at the expense of another. To improve their finances, domains tried to improve their trade balances through import substitution and export promotion policies. Over time, the domain's "national interest" (kokueki) came to be defined, in addition to domestic prosperity, in terms of competitiveness with other domains.

Kaiho Seiryō (1755–1817) was one of the leading advocates of a strategic economic policy for domains. Kaiho studied Sorai's Ancient Learning and Dutch Studies. He then spent his career traveling from domain to domain conducting surveys of geography, resources, production, and local practices. As something of a management consultant for daimyo, Kaiho became known for his advocacy of domain monopoly control of specialized products to promote the daimyo's kokueki.[31]

Like Dazai, Kaiho saw nothing wrong with domains getting involved in commercial affairs. Indeed, he saw trade as a part of the natural order of things:

> Field, mountain, sea, gold, and rice are all goods between heaven and earth that are bought and sold. That goods bear other goods is a natural principle. There is no difference between gold bearing interest and a field bearing rice. Mountains bearing lumber, the sea bearing fish and salt, gold and rice bearing interest are all according to the principles of heaven and earth.[32]

Starting with the Confucian notion of natural principle, Kaiho argued that the difference between commercial gain and agricultural prosperity was not as great as others suggested. Even money lending occurred within the parameters of natural principle. The ruler, then, should not hesitate in promoting commerce as another part of the natural order he was entrusted by heaven to govern.

But Kaiho took this line of reasoning a step further than most of his contemporaries did. He saw trade as not only acceptable, but also essential in the context of the domains' competitive relationships with one another.

In his "Advice on Practice" (*Keikodan*) written near the end of his life in 1813, Kaiho argued that trade had replaced warfare between domains under the Pax Tokugawa, but the stakes of the competition remained high:

> This is an age when one must not let his guard down toward other domains and must carefully cultivate his own country. One must be on guard not from his neighbor's violent attack, but rather from loss through trade . . . If a domain does not innovate to increase its land's produce relative to its neighbors, the neighbor will grow rich and the domain will grow poor. And if the neighbor becomes prosperous and the domain is impoverished, gold and silver will flow to the prosperous land.[33]

This vision of economic interaction as a competition akin to warfare was important for several reasons. First, it equated economic competition with military competition for power between states. Where the physiocratic view had disparaged mercantile activity, Kaiho elevated trade to a matter of survival. Second, thinking of trade as a form of war brought commerce to the center of domain politics. Economic policy was consequently judged less upon vague moral principles than on its concrete contribution to improving the domains' trade balances. Third, the domain states began to take an activist approach to economic affairs. No longer content to leave commerce to merchants, domain officials took a leadership role in technology acquisition and other measures to promote commercial advantage.

In practice, daimyo in the late eighteenth century responded to their financial crises with new commercial policies including domain monopolies of specialized regional products. Kumamoto domain, for example, imported techniques for producing silk from Nishijin in Kyoto and promoted wax tree cultivation through interest-free loans to farmers. Yonezawa imported silkworms and advisers from Date and Fukushima. Kaga provided tax exemptions to lacquer ware and gold leaf industries.[34]

Recent scholarship has shown that merchants were also important in the formation of a new economic ideology. Tetsuo Najita's work on the *Kaitokudō*, a merchant academy in Osaka, demonstrates that merchants were active in Confucian discourse on virtue.[35] In his study of the rise of *kokueki* thinking in Tosa, Luke Roberts argues that merchants used the concept of the realm's interest to justify their activities as legitimate service to the community. He concludes that *kokueki* was a negotiated concept with which the daimyo and merchants entered a symbiotic relationship. By allowing more commercial activity in the name of the realm's interest, the daimyo increased his revenue. With improved social status and legitimacy, the merchants could pursue a wider range of profitable ventures.[36]

Honda Toshiaki (1744–1820) carried this strategic economic thinking from the domain level to Japan as a whole and used European mercantilist texts to support his views. He was from Echigo in northeast Japan, studied astronomy and mathematics in Edo, and took an interest in Chinese translations of European books.[37] From his studies, Honda concluded that Japan should emulate some of the mercantilist practices of the European powers. In his *A Secret Plan of Government*, Honda proposed a change in Japan's guiding model:

> China does not merit being used as a model. Since Japan is a maritime nation, shipping and trade should be the chief concern of the ruler. Ships should be sent to all countries to obtain products needed for national consumption and to bring precious metals to Japan. A maritime nation is equipped with the means to increase her national strength.[38]

This passage had momentous implications. Chinese culture and institutions had been a profound influence on Japanese political and economic thought for a thousand years. Now Honda was suggesting that this long tradition be discarded in favor of a new model that he believed was more appropriate to Japan's circumstances. The Tokugawa who enacted the seclusion policy would hardly have called Japan a "maritime nation," but Honda clearly believed that Japan had much in common with England and Holland, small countries that became wealthy through commerce.

In opposition to the Tokugawa regime's restrictions on international trade, Honda was clearly advocating that the Japanese state should be active in promoting trade with the outside world. Moreover, this trade should be conducted with a mercantilist strategy to advance the accumulation of specie.

The similarities between Honda's view of Japan in international trade and the *kokueki* view of the domain's trade within the Tokugawa system are obvious. In both formulations, the ruler should use state resources to actively promote trade. Wealth and strength were defined in terms of specie. The main objective of trade, therefore, was the maximization of gold and silver in the ruler's treasury.

This view of the economy was very different from the Western liberal conception of economics as the aggregate of individual profit maximizing choices. In Tokugawa Japan, the people produced for the benefit of the realm either at the domain or at the national level. The realm's interest was defined *ipso facto* as the lord's interest. Although the ruler, in theory, had a moral obligation to show benevolence to the individual, the individual had no inherent right to the profits of his or her labor. In practice, this meant that commoners were resources to be managed for the maximum production of revenue for the lord.

We see this view of state management of economic activity clearly in Honda's thought. Although Honda supported increased international trade, he maintained the Confucian belief that it could not be left to commoners. On this point, Honda wrote,

> Shipping and foreign trade are the responsibility of the ruler and should not be left to the merchants. If shipping is left entirely in the hands of merchants, they act as their greed and evil purposes dictate, thereby disturbing commodity prices throughout the country.[39]

Honda continued the conventional Confucian view that "greed and evil purposes" were the merchant's sole motivation. To avoid this problem, the ruler should take the lead in establishing foreign trade. In this, we can see an early conception of the state as the only actor in the economy who had the community's best interest in mind. All others were simply motivated by a greedy lust for profits. The state, according to Honda, should institute mercantilist policies including political centralization, central control of the circulation of money, universal education and technical training, and promotion of overseas trade.[40]

Conclusion

By the late eighteenth century, important changes were occurring in the Tokugawa Confucian understanding of the state's proper relationship to economic activity. To meet the challenges of commercialization and the resulting financial crises, daimyo looked for new sources of revenue. Intellectuals responded to these conditions with new approaches to political economy. Thinkers argued that commerce was just another tool of statecraft with which the ruler could fulfill his moral obligation under Confucian doctrine to "order the realm and save the people" and promote the "domain's interest." Upon this fundamental philosophical justification of state activism in trade and commerce, intellectuals elaborated a mercantile vision of economic affairs in which the ruler had to safeguard his own domain's interest in its competition with other domains in the Tokugawa system. Scholars of Western texts extended this view to the national level, arguing that Japan's ruling authorities should actively promote commerce with foreign nations.

This view of a state-guided political economy was the basis of a form of early industrial policy that a number of domains pursued. The *tozama* daimyo that traditionally chafed under Tokugawa hegemony were among the most successful in promoting their domains' products. Satsuma, one of these successful *tozama* domains, became home to some of the most important leaders in Japan's Meiji transition to capitalism.

CHAPTER 2

Confucian Moralism and Economic Realism in Satsuma

One of the domains to make the ideological adjustments necessary to take economic reforms seriously was Satsuma in southwestern Japan. When Ōkubo Toshimichi, one of the most important architects of the Meiji state's economic policy, was born in Satsuma in 1830, the domain was in serious financial trouble. Spontaneous commercial development during the Tokugawa period generally passed by the domain of Satsuma. Situated in the southwest corner of Kyushu, Satsuma was far from the political center in Edo and commercial centers in Kyoto and Osaka. A high proportion of samurai to commoners and the domain's deliberate efforts to constrain commerce further aggravated the disadvantages of geographic isolation.

Commercial backwardness and growing expenses combined to create a crisis in Satsuma in the late eighteenth century. To combat these problems, the domain bureaucracy under daimyo Shimazu Shigehide (1745–1833) tried to increase the production of Satsuma's particularly lucrative goods. Natural disasters and Shigehide's high levels of spending eroded any gains that were made in commerce. Seeking a solution to his dilemma, Shigehide's ministers consulted with Satō Nobuhiro (1769–1850), a scholar from the northeastern domain of Dewa who opened a school in Edo in the late Tokugawa period becoming well-known as an agricultural specialist and political economist. In 1827, Shigehide put Zusho Hirosato (1776–1848) in charge of Satsuma finances and Zusho instituted a series of successful economic reforms based on Satō's principles. These reforms erased Satsuma's formidable debt and turned its monopoly enterprises into profitable ventures. By the time Westerners in the 1840s began seeking a trade treaty with the

Ryūkyū Islands, Satsuma was becoming one of the wealthiest domains in Japan. Satsuma leaders would later use this wealth to topple the shogun and promote Japan's modernization after the Meiji Restoration. Since key Meiji economic policy makers such as Ōkubo Toshimichi (1830–1878), Godai Tomoatsu (1835–1885), Matsukata Masayoshi (1835–1924), Kuroda Kiyotaka (1840–1900), and Maeda Masana (1850–1921) all had their formative experiences as Satsuma officials, it is crucial to understand the evolution of economic thought and policy in Satsuma.

Satsuma on the Periphery of the Tokugawa System

Satsuma was one of the largest domains in the Tokugawa political system and its ruling Shimazu family was among the most powerful of the *tozama* daimyo. Although they and their allies lost the decisive Battle of Sekigahara to the Tokugawa in 1600, the Shimazu maintained control of their ancestral territory in southwestern Kyushu throughout the Edo period.

The Shimazu first came to power in 1185 when the Kamakura shogunate appointed Shimazu Tadahisa (Unknown–1227) as the military governor of Satsuma. During the Warring States period (1467–1568), the Shimazu conquered most of the island of Kyushu. By 1587, however, Hideyoshi's forces had pushed them back to their holdings in Satsuma, Ōsumi, and Hyūga, which were roughly the same area as today's Kagoshima prefecture.[1] In 1592, Shimazu Yoshihiro (1535–1619) participated in Hideyoshi's invasion of Korea.[2] After Hideyoshi's death in 1598, Japanese forces withdrew from Korea and Yoshihiro brought home captive Korean artisans to teach the technology behind their delicate porcelain to Satsuma potters. This pottery came to be known in Japan as "Satsuma ware" (*Satsuma yaki*) and became one of the domain's most important industries.[3]

As *tozama* daimyo, "outer lords" who opposed Tokugawa Ieyasu at Sekigahara, the Shimazu were excluded from holding office in the shogun's central government, but Satsuma's size and power allowed the Shimazu family to escape the land confiscation and other reprisals that befell lesser domains. Satsuma was also untouched by several of the Tokugawa control measures designed to pacify the countryside. Where samurai in other areas were withdrawn from the countryside into castle towns and paid stipends rather than receiving fiefs of land, many Satsuma samurai remained in control of peasant villages and the Shimazu continued to grant fiefs to subordinates in charge of regional administration. Satsuma was even able to circumvent the Tokugawa's attempt to control trade between Japan and other countries by establishing a suzerain relationship with the Ryūkyū Kingdom and by using the islands as an intermediary for overseas trade.

Perhaps Satsuma's most important distinctive political feature was its high concentration of samurai. Losing some of their lands to Hideyoshi and the Tokugawa, the Shimazu family's retainers had to move to the region around Kagoshima. By 1874, the ratio of samurai to commoners was one to three compared with the Japan wide average of one to seventeen.[4]

To bring order to Japan near the end of the Warring States period, samurai in many areas were forced to leave their fiefs in the countryside and reside in central castle towns where they could be more closely monitored. Hideyoshi's "sword hunt" policy in the 1580s accelerated this trend by disarming commoners and restricting samurai access to peasant villages. This had the effect of sharpening a distinction between the warrior class and the peasant class that had been much more fluid during the Warring States period. In 1615, Tokugawa Ieyasu decreed that each domain should have only one castle and abolish all other fortifications.

Satsuma's size, power, and distance from Japan's political centers allowed the Shimazu to largely ignore these mandates. Samurai remained dispersed throughout the territory. Outlying fortifications controlled entry and movement within the domain and officials were able to keep the domain largely secluded while controlling the flow of trade and information.[5] Regions within Satsuma had their own castles, were semi-autonomous, and were required to be self-sufficient in their grain production. Regional lords controlled fiefs and maintained their own samurai retainers whom they were ready to lead in battle in the Shimazu's service. The Shimazu controlled their vassals with a series of measures quite similar to those used by the Tokugawa in the rest of Japan. Regional lords were required to reside in Kagoshima and leave hostages when they returned to their home regions, which were scattered among other lands under direct Shimazu control. The presence of a high proportion of samurai in the countryside gave Satsuma the dubious distinction as "the country where there are no peasant uprisings." In fact, there were only two known major disturbances, the Kaseda uprising and the Intabu riot.[6]

The 102 administrative districts that the Shimazu controlled directly were called *gō*. Each *gō* had an administrative center at the site of original outer castle. The Shimazu dispatched a manager (*jitō*) to administer the district and the warriors (*gōshi*) who resided there. To gain self-sufficiency, both regional lords and Shimazu managers used samurai to actively administer their lands. Low ranking samurai, untouched by Hideyoshi's reforms, farmed the land during peacetime as they had since

Kamakura reforms. These *gōshi* were also required to be self-sufficient and instead of a salary were given small plots of land to cultivate. It was often difficult to make a living and some *gōshi* were so impoverished that they were given special permission to engage in commerce and handicrafts to supplement their incomes.[7] In fact, there were so many samurai that according to the *Geographic Survey of Satsuma, Ōsumi, and Hyūga*, the eleven districts of Nagatoshigō, Irikigō, Kurokigō, Imutagō, Kamōgō, Kiyomizugō, Ichinarigō, Masakigō, Shimomitsumatagō, Ayagō, and Sugigō had more samurai than commoners.[8] The ideal of self-sufficient farmer-soldiers often proved to be elusive as *gōshi* households were rarely as efficient as peasants specializing in farming.

Merchants and fishermen lived in specially designated communities that samurai officials also controlled. These commercial towns were not very widespread. Of the 102 *gō* in Satsuma, 57 did not have any commercial town at all. If a merchant family did manage to make a gain through some profitable commercial venture, the domain government extracted it in the form of contributions.[9] Nearly all products fell under the direct or indirect control of the state monopoly system. Reports of fire damage give us some idea of what goods were being produced in the early nineteenth century. A fire in 1808 occurring in Shimomachi, one of the three districts surrounding the Shimazu headquarters at Tsurumaru castle, damaged the pawnshop and dealers of *shōchū*, liquor, sake, oil, hair cosmetics, cosmetics, mis made from been curd, soy sauce, sesame seeds, kitchenware and sundries, wood, cotton cloth, vegetables, and fish. A report from 1845 lists damage to shops selling rice, clothing, medicines, nightsoil, paper, and metal goods.[10] Although regulated by the domain, markets did arise to supply basic needs.

State control even extended to the people's personal lives. Marriages between the classes were prohibited and other interactions were strictly regulated. Merchants were restricted from travel to peasant villages except for the sale of essential items. The fact that the commercialization that had swept much of Japan from the Genroku period in the late seventeenth century had not penetrated Satsuma very deeply was also a testament to Satsuma's isolated geographic position on the periphery of the Tokugawa political economy and to the relative strength of its feudal institutions. These factors led Robert Sakai to conclude, "The non-development of commerce may be attributed to the lack of a developed money economy, the strict regulations against travel, and the bias of Confucian statecraft against private mercantilism."[11]

Commercial gain to benefit the state, however, was another matter. When the domain ran into financial difficulties in the mid-Tokugawa period, domain officials tried to find ways to monopolize products for the domain's profit. They seem to have been aware that commerce needed to be exploited to strengthen the state, but were also wary of the potential deleterious effects that commercial wealth in private hands might have on the state's power.

One of the earliest ways that Satsuma officials attempted to augment the domain's commercial wealth was through its special relationship with the Kingdom of Ryūkyū in what is present day Okinawa prefecture. According to the "History of the Shimazu's Territory" (*Shimazu kokushi*), the first Ryūkyū envoy to visit Satsuma to seek friendly relations arrived in 1481.[12] A military expedition in 1609 finally established Satsuma control over Ryūkyū foreign trade. This connection was kept secret at first because in the mid-sixteenth century, Chinese merchants had been prohibited from trading with the Japanese, whom the Ming court considered pirates.[13] Indeed, the Shimazu had high hopes of establishing a monopoly over trade with the Chinese through the Ryūkyū Islands as long as the Ming refused to trade with Japan proper after Hideyoshi's invasion attempts.[14]

In his study of Tokugawa foreign relations, Ronald Toby shows that the late seventeenth-century Ryūkyū Kingdom maintained tributary relations with the Chinese emperor, Satsuma daimyo, and Tokugawa shogun simultaneously. "For each new [Ryūkyūan] king, while he expressed his fealty to China, and received investiture from the Chinese emperor, also owed his installation in office to Japanese benefice, from both the shogun and the daimyo of Satsuma."[15] Although the Ryūkyū Kingdom had more than one overlord, Satsuma by virtue of proximity and interest in Ryūkyū affairs seems to have played the most active role.

Between 1612 and 1622, the Ryūkyū Kingdom under Satsuma orders dispatched five tribute missions to China in spite of a Ming decree that they occur only once per decade. In addition to these official tribute missions to the court, other ships were sent with tokens of the Ryūkyū Kingdom's esteem for the Chinese emperor. In fact, Satsuma leaders encouraged the Ryūkyūans to use every chance they could find to send tribute missions for trade including coronations, weddings, birthdays, funerals, and New Year celebrations.[16]

The Tokugawa shogunate knew of Satsuma's trade with China through the Ryūkyū Islands and even encouraged it during the Ming ban on official trade with Japan. In the decades before and after the Qing's defeat of the Ming in 1644, political instability in the Asian continent disrupted trade. Due to a shortage of Chinese goods, especially silk and medicine, the shogunate ordered Satsuma to obtain these goods.

In 1684, however, the Qing began to allow official trade with Japan. Chinese trade with the shogunate at Nagasaki removed the need for Ryūkyū intermediation.[17]

Indeed, the shogunate tried to extend the seclusion policy to Satsuma. In 1683, the shogunate prohibited Satsuma from selling woolen products that competed with the Tokugawa licensed merchants in Nagasaki. These items were made in Europe and came to the Ryūkyū Islands through China. In 1687, the shogunate limited the value of tribute trade to 804 *kan* of silver for tribute ships and 402 *kan* for envoy-returning ships. In 1714, these amounts were reduced to 604 *kan* and 302 *kan*.[18] These restrictions were further aggravated by the shogunate's debasement of its coinage. With the amount of coins available for export fixed, this devaluation meant that fewer Chinese goods could be bought for import. This shortage of coins forced Satsuma officials to look for new goods to export to China. In 1691, a trading mission tried to purchase silk with camphor, *konbu* (kelp), shark fins, shellfish, soy sauce, and seaweed.[19]

In 1789, the shogunate prohibited Satsuma from selling foreign products other than raw silk and silk damask outside of the domain to prevent Satsuma from competing with the Tokugawa's own monopoly on foreign trade that grew out of the "closed country" policy. By 1837, Satsuma was forbidden to sell any goods. This restriction was gradually relaxed as the shogunate weakened and by 1846, the shogunate permitted the sale of sixteen products as long as their value did not exceed 1,200 *kan* of silver.[20]

The Satsuma daimyo maintained control over commerce with the Ryūkyūs primarily by allocating currency for use in transactions with the Chinese. In fact, only authorized Ryūkyūans could even possess Japanese money. Satsuma officials also closely inspected the contents of ships returning from China. While being prepared for shipment to Satsuma, goods were heavily guarded to prevent their illegal sale.[21]

Although the Ryūkyū trade may not have been very quantitatively significant in the overall picture of Satsuma finances, it did provide domain officials with important international trade experience. This added to the stock of knowledge that Satsuma samurai derived from their direct administration of agriculture and commerce within the domain.

Satsuma's high concentration of samurai prevented the growth of self-governing villages that developed in many regions where the samurai had been withdrawn from the land to the castle town. The state reached deep into Satsuma society and used its power to enforce ideological conformity.

Satsuma forces participated in the suppression of the Shimabara Rebellion in 1637 and supported the shogunate's subsequent suppression of Christianity. From 1635, every person was listed in a population registry. Men and women had to carry a small wooded tablet listing their names and religious affiliation. These measures were also used against the Buddhist Ikkō sect that held the authority of its teaching above temporal rulers. Oda Nobunaga, Toyotomi Hideyoshi, and Tokugawa Ieyasu all faced resistance from Ikkō uprisings, so the sect was banned.[22]

In sum, Satsuma in the early eighteenth century was perhaps the last place we would expect to produce leaders who might embrace modern capitalism. It had a relatively large hereditary elite that jealously guarded its privileges, however meager in many cases, against upstarts from other classes. The domain state tried to keep its oversupply of samurai busy through administrative posts that reached down to the most mundane aspects of daily life. To maintain their position, these administrative samurai had a strong incentive to tightly regulate economic activity that might erode the social hierarchy by transferring wealth to the lower classes. Domain officials were also concerned with enforcing the ideological underpinnings of their rule and ruthlessly suppressed creeds that claimed an authority higher than that of the daimyo.

The strength of Satsuma's feudal institutions had important implications for the economic ideology that developed there. Economic expansion and development of natural resources would have to be justified by their contributions to the sovereign's interests in maintaining order. The samurai elite, rather than commoners, would have to take the initiative in advocating policy changes if proposals were to have any chance for adoption. Reforms would be conceived as new methods for managing the realm's resources to improve the domain state's wealth and power both at home and relative to other domains in the Tokugawa system.

Daimyo Shimazu Shigehide's Financial Crises

After his father Shigetoshi died in 1755, Shimazu Shigehide, at the age of eleven, became the twenty-fifth daimyo of Satsuma (see table 2.1). His grandfather Shimazu Tsugutoyo had retired in 1746 due to illness, but he advised young Shigehide until his own death in 1760. During Shigehide's tenure as daimyo, Satsuma experienced severe financial difficulties. When he was old enough to govern on his own, Shigehide patronized studies of European texts mainly in the fields of science and medicine. Shigehide's involvement in Western learning was more of a hobby than a concerted effort to import Western institutions. Buying

Table 2.1 The Shimazu Daimyo of Satsuma

Daimyo	Life	Reign	Important Adviser(s)
Shigehide	1745–1833	1755–1787	
Narinobu	1773–1841	1787–1808	Shigehide
Narioki	1789–1859	1808–1851	Shigehide
			Zusho Hirosato
Nariakira	1809–1858	1851–1858	Saigō Takamori
			Ōkubo Toshimichi
Tadayoshi	1840–1897	1858–1869	Narioki
			Hisamitsu

foreign books proved to be rather expensive and Shigehide's spending left the domain treasury in an even worse condition. Nevertheless, future Satsuma leaders could build upon the technical knowledge gained in Shigehide's early patronage of Western scholarship.

Like many samurai leaders, Shigehide began his intellectual journey with the orthodox Zhu Xi School of Confucianism. He studied with scholars such as Yamada Kunhyō and Kuniyama Sonshi who traced their intellectual lineages to Muro Kyūsō (1658–1734), a Confucian scholar in Edo who had given lectures to the shogun in 1711 translated a widely circulated Chinese primer on Confucian virtue as *Riku yuengi taii*.[23] Interestingly, this book came to the shogun's attention after a Confucian scholar from the Ryūkyūs named Tei Junsoku had the work published in China at his own expense and it circulated back to Japan via Satsuma's trade with the Ryūkyū Kingdom.[24] What might otherwise be just a historical footnote illustrates that the flow of scholarly work was much wider in East Asia than the Tokugawa's official seclusion policy would lead us to believe.

In the spring of 1769, Kuniyama Sonshi prepared a primer entitled "The Way of the Gentleman" (*kundō*) on the Confucian ethics of ruling the domain. It held up not only the ancient Chinese sages, but also the Shimazu ancestors Tadayoshi and Yoshihiro as moral exemplars who had brought order to their realms. The work extolled the virtues of performing one's duty in the Confucian five personal relationships of ruler–subject, husband–wife, father–son, older–younger brother, and friend-friend. Its major focus was on the importance of the role of classical education in the marking of a wise and effective ruler.[25]

From long ago, men without learning who deserve the title of wise ruler have been few. What a joy it is to draw near to the nature of the sages from the beginning and understand the similarities with ourselves so the wisdom that comes from knowledge can guide us in correct action! However, most of those who occupy the places of prestige and wealth in this world become indolent and indulge in songs and women without giving any thought to governing the country and without even hearing an outline of the works of the sages.[26]

This passage is typical of Zhu Xi's perspective on education that Kuniyama would have certainly learned from the Muro Kyūsō school. In his preface to *The Great Learning by Chapter and Verse*, Zhu Xi wrote,

> The Book of the *Great Learning* comprises the method by which people were taught the higher learning of antiquity. When Heaven gives birth to the people, it gives each one, without exception, a nature of humaneness, rightness, ritual decorum, and wisdom. They could not, however, be equal in their physical endowments, and thus do not all have the capacity to know what that nature consists in or how to preserve it whole. Once someone appears among them who is intelligent and wise, and able to fully develop his nature, Heaven is sure to commission him as ruler and teacher of the myriad peoples, so that, being governed and instructed, they may be able to recover their original nature . . .
>
> With the decline of the Zhou, sage and worthy rulers no longer appeared and the school system was not well maintained. The transformation of the people through education became eclipsed and popular customs deteriorated. At that time the sage Confucius appeared, but being unable to attain the position of ruler–teacher by which to carry out government and education, he could do no more than recite the ways of the sage kings and pass them along, in order to make them known to later generations.[27]

Here we see the Satsuma daimyo Shigehide embracing the Confucian notion that a ruler's legitimacy rested on the inherently superior nature bestowed upon him by Heaven. The ruler then had a moral obligation to cultivate his own nature through classical learning and to promote the instruction of his people in the way of the sages. Knowledge was to be cultivated both through the empirical investigation of the world and through introspection into one's own personal nature. As Zhu Xi wrote in his notes on the *Great Learning*,

> Hence the learner as he comes upon the things of this world must proceed from principles already known and further fathom until he reaches the limit. After exerting himself for a long time, he will one day experience a breakthrough to integral comprehension. Then the qualities of all things

whether internal or external, refined or coarse, will all be apprehended and the mind, in its whole substance and great functioning, will all be clearly manifested. This is "things [having been] investigated." This is the utmost of knowing.[28]

This passage generated considerable debate over the nature of knowledge in the Confucian world of East Asia. Rationalists tended to emphasize the deductive approach of beginning with first principles and then using reason to arrive at specific conclusions. This had the political implication of legitimating the status quo as constructed by sages according to natural principles ordained by Heaven. Empiricists, on the other hand, focused on the "investigation of things" and argued that an inductive approach should be taken, in which specific observations and experience lead to an understanding of more general principles. Intellectual and political leaders could lean either to the rationalist or the empiricist side of Neo-Confucianism depending on the ideological needs of their times. Conservatives could legitimate the status quo as the product of universal principle, whereas reformers might argue that a thorough "investigation of things" suggested that existing ordering principles no longer fit observed reality.

Zen Buddhism was another element in the Japanese intellectual tradition that emphasized empirical observation of reality rather than abstract speculation and rational deduction from first principles. Shigehide took a clear interest in Zen and visited scholars at Manpukuji, a temple in the Ōbaku School of Zen in the mountains near Kyoto.[29] Zen had been popular among the warrior class as a method to train the mind to face death fearlessly. It was also manifested in martial arts, tea ceremony, ink painting, and calligraphy in which the practitioner ideally practiced to the point where sophisticated techniques could be performed without thought. Zen philosophy was suspicious of rational thought and the Rinzai sect attempted to overcome the constantly scheming rational mind through meditation on kōan conundrums, which would hopefully lead to the sudden realization that nothing permanent exists and all is an illusion. In this way, Zen formed an important counterbalance to the rationalist Neo-Confucian emphasis of enduring universal principles.

For Shigehide, empirical observations soon began to run counter to his Confucian ideals. Like many other domains in the Tokugawa system, Satsuma's financial conditions worsened after the Genroku era. The cost of the alternate attendance system and other obligations to the bakufu weighed heavily on the domain treasury. For example, in 1754, the Tokugawa bakufu ordered Satsuma to dispatch 1,000 men and make financial contributions for the construction of irrigation works on the Kisogawa River. When this project was complete, the domain's debt stood at 886,000 gold *ryō*, a considerable sum.[30] Satsuma's financial obligations to the Tokugawa weighed heavily upon the Satsuma treasury again in 1789 when the eleventh shogun Tokugawa Ienari took Shigehide's daughter as his wife. The expense of the processional to Edo, gifts, and ceremonies further increased Satsuma's domainal debt.[31]

Bad luck also played a part in worsening Satsuma's finances. During Shigehide's reign, several fires and natural disasters severely taxed the domain administration's economic means. The year he became daimyo, 3,000 people starved to death on Tokunoshima despite aid shipments of rice from Kagoshima. Later the domain residence in Edo was damaged in a fire. Typhoons and insect blights took their toll on agricultural land. An epidemic in Nakanojima killed 1,700 people. In 1779, the volcano on Sakurajima, just off the coast from the domain capital Kagoshima, erupted resulting in many casualties and severe crop damage.[32] Therefore while Shigehide was daimyo, Satsuma was in a state of financial decline, which increased pressure on the ruling elite to find new and creative solutions to the domain's economic problems.

In 1771, Shigehide obtained bakufu permission to visit the Dutch trading mission at Deshima in Nagasaki. The Dutch were allowed to maintain the strictly regulated outpost as an exception to the general Tokugawa policy preventing Japanese interaction with Westerners. In the early eighteenth century, the shogun permitted the circulation of Dutch texts and soon Japanese scholars of Dutch Learning (*rangaku*) were studying Western geography, science, and particularly medicine. Shigehide soon developed a deep interest in Dutch Learning and Particularly medicine. Shigehide soon developed a deep interest in Dutch Learning and established institutions in Satsuma to engage in further research. He worked with the scholar of Dutch Matsumura Genkō and apparently gained some proficiency in the Dutch language, at least well enough to keep a diary in the foreign script. He soon tried to integrate Western knowledge into samurai training in Satsuma. He established the Zōshikan and Enbukan schools to encourage literary and martial arts. He also erected a medical school to train physicians and conduct medical research. In 1779, he added the Meijikan and Tenmonkan for the study of astronomy. Outside Kagoshima, he ordered the cultivation of herb gardens in Yoshino, Yamagawa, and Sata to grow medicinal plants. He also compiled a study of medicinal plants in the Ryūkyū and Yaku Islands.[33] All these intellectual endeavors costed money and the domain's economic fortunes continued to decline. Later Satsuma leaders would use

Shigehide's advances in Dutch Studies to improve the economy, but in Shigehide's lifetime, there was very little material payoff.

Although it is difficult to judge whether historical figures really believed the ideas to which they were exposed, Shigehide did seem to see himself as a model Confucian ruler in his patronage of scholarship and education. Records show a purchase in 1767 of over one hundred volumes including Confucian works, Chinese history, and Chinese poetry collections. He also owned many Japanese works from as early as the tenth century *Kokinshū* and several other collections of *waka* poetry. Of particular interest was a work entitled *Tsūshōkō*, which probably refers to "Thoughts on Chinese and Barbarian Commerce" (*Kai Tsūshōkō*). This work by the Nagasaki merchant Nishikawa Gotomi described the customs, people, and products of China, Korea, Taiwan, the Philippines, Holland, and England.[34]

At first, Shigehide's approach to economic problems was decidedly fundamentalist. He levied special taxes on the peasants and on samurai stipends. In 1768, he made sumptuary decrees that soup would henceforth be made with only one vegetable instead of two and that tea should always be used twice. He also continued the practice of promoting land reclamation projects to increase agricultural production. In 1768 and 1777, Shigehide appropriated 10,000 *koku* to reclaim land for dry fields and fields for collecting salt from seawater.[35]

When traditional modes of boosting revenue and cutting expenses failed to have much effect, he turned to reorganizing the domain monopolies. The domain government had, for some time, encouraged peasants to produce goods for the domain to sell to the rest of Japan. Sugar was the most profitable of these since only the southern islands under Satsuma control had the climate to grow sugar cane.

Domain officials "bought" sugar from the peasants on the sugar producing islands with rice. Satsuma officials determined the exchange rate of sugar to rice. The allotted quota commanded a price of 0.35 *shō* of rice per *kin* of sugar and supplementary production received 0.4 *shō* per *kin*. Thus, there was an incentive for the peasants to exceed their quota. By 1745, cultivators on Ōshima had almost completely shifted from growing rice to raising sugar cane. Merchants were not allowed to set foot on the sugar islands, so the peasants had to purchase necessities from the domain.[36]

Shigehide used samurai to manage the domain's commercial interests in the sugar monopoly. As figure 2.1 indicates, these administrators were quite successful in increasing production (or at extracting it from the peasants).

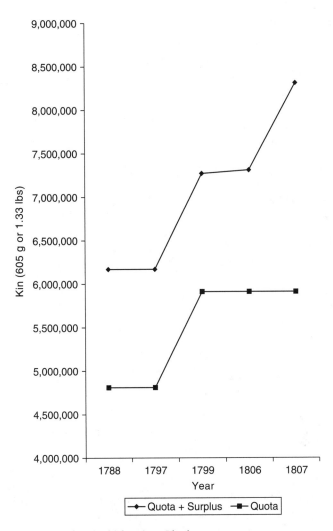

Figure 2.1 Output of Satsuma's Three Sugar Islands

Source: Matsui Masatō, *Satsuma hanshū Shimazu Shigehide* (Tokyo: Honpō shoseki, 1985), 138.

To secure more revenue for the domain government from agricultural and commercial sources, Shigehide had to carry out administrative reform. Each *gō* was highly organized with peasants and commercial communities under the watchful eye of the *gōshi* samurai. Shigehide dispatched castle town samurai to inspect conditions at the local level.

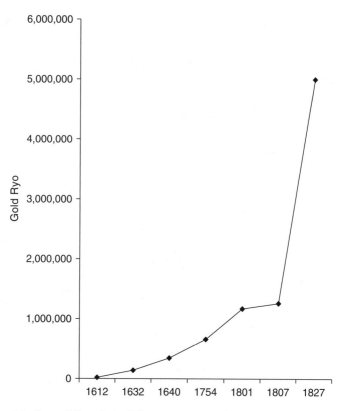

Figure 2.2   Satsuma's Skyrocketing Debt

Source: Data from Haraguchi Torao, *Bakumatsu Satsuma: Higeki no kaikakusha, Zusho Shōzaemon, Chūkō shinsho 101* (Tokyo: Chūō Kōron sha, 1966), 67.

A 1768 law held these directors personally responsible for the output of the *gō* under their supervision.[37] In this way, Shigehide's policies further developed the bureaucratic machinery to carry out central economic planning and control. But, in spite of Shigehide's efforts, Satsuma's debt continued to grow as is apparent from figure 2.2.

Shigehide retired in 1789 and his son Narinobu became daimyo. Yet Shigehide continued to exercise much influence on domain policies. After his retirement, some criticized, what they considered, frivolous expenditures on hobbies and Dutch Studies. Narinobu had domain elders Kazan Hisanobu and Chichibu Kiho conduct a study and make recommendations on how to relieve the domain's financial distress. Their report, "Record of

Thoughts on Matters Close at Hand," (*Kinshiroku*) followed the Confucian moral principles of showing benevolence to the people and encouraging frugality in government. Unnecessary personnel were to be eliminated from the domain bureaucracy and Shigehide's programs were to be cut.[38]

Shigehide considered the supporters of the proposed reforms to be "without loyalty and without filial piety," which was a very serious charge according to Confucian doctrine. In 1808, Kazan and Chichibu were dismissed and ordered to commit ritual suicide (*seppuku*) along with thirty of their followers. Shigehide exiled another hundred or so to the islands. He even forced his son Narinobu into retirement and replaced him with his grandson Narioki in 1809.[39]

Although Shigehide was willing to entertain alternative sources of practical knowledge and took an increasingly realist approach to economic matters, his understanding of political and moral propriety remained thoroughly Confucian. His solutions to financial problems were ultimately designed to reinforce state power and traditional social hierarchies. On one hand, he introduced Western science to Satsuma and used it to find new products and improve old ones. On the other, he increased the power of the central domain bureaucracy over the regional lords and *gōshi* and gave it a wider mandate to manage economic activity.

In spite of these efforts, Satsuma's financial position continued to worsen. The Ryūkyū trade had fallen off considerably by the early nineteenth century. High prices coupled with Shigehide's expenditures increased Satsuma's budget deficit and its debt grew each year. Perhaps in desperation near the end of his life, Shigehide authorized soliciting the advice of Satō Nobuhiro one of the leading political economists of the time.

Satō Nobuhiro's State-Centered Vision of Political Economy

The growing financial crisis in many domains during the late eighteenth and early nineteenth centuries encouraged new lines of inquiry in Confucian statecraft. Several scholars achieved wide recognition as experts in this field and traveled from domain to domain offering advice to daimyo who wished to improve their financial positions. One of the most important of these traveling consultants was Satō Nobuhiro from whom Satsuma officials solicited assistance in the late 1820s.

Satō was from Dewa in northeast Japan. His family had studied Chinese medicine in the early Tokugawa period, but when they fell on hard times, they turned to researching the problems of agricultural management. In 1784, Satō went to Edo to study astronomy and Dutch

Learning. He later became a follower of Hirata Atsutane's Shintō revivalist "National Learning" (*kokugaku*) school.[40]

From this background, he developed a holistic economic policy characterized by militant nationalism, strong central control, and careful exploitation of Japan's agricultural, commercial, and industrial resources to fulfill its divinely ordained role to bring order to the world. In Satō, Satsuma officials found a kindred spirit and his writings confirmed and gave intellectual sophistication to the policy direction that they had already chosen.

Satō's acceptance of the National Learning view of Japan's mythic origins and historical destiny was important for several reasons. First, it gave economic activity and the state's management of it a higher status than Confucian statecraft did. Moreover, the idea of national destiny suggested change and development as history unfolded. Finally, the nativists' discussion of Japan as distinct from China and Western countries helped to fuel a growing sense of unique identity that would become an important component of Japanese nationalism in the late nineteenth century.

After the Genroku period (1688–1704) of economic expansion, the bakufu and domains were plagued with financial troubles and political disturbances. The Nativist school emerged around scholars advocating a return to direct rule by the emperor. The rise of the Nativist school coincided with the growth of Dutch Studies. In 1720, the shogun Tokugawa Yoshimune allowed Dutch books to circulate in Japan as long as they did not contain references to Christianity. As these Dutch books increased the Japanese intellectual elite's understanding of conditions in the world beyond East Asia, scholars such as Motoori Norinaga and Hirata Atsutane revived the study of the Shintō myths in the eighth century *Kojiki* (Record of Ancient Matters) and *Nihon Shoki* (Chronicles of Japan) to redefine Japanese identity and sense of mission. As Motoori wrote, "The 'special dispensation of our Imperial Land' means that ours is the native land of the Heaven-Shining Goddess who casts her light over all countries in the four seas."[41] From Motoori's view of Japan's special dispensation, we see two important ideas that colored Satō's ideas of political economy. First, the gods looked with favor upon Japan, which in turn had a destiny to enlighten the rest of the world. Second, agriculture was the foundation of the economy upon which all else depended.

Hirata echoed Motoori's notion of Japan's divine status, "Japan is thus the homeland of the gods, and that is why we call it the Land of the Gods. This is a matter of universal belief, and is quite beyond dispute."[42] This emphasis on Japan as the wellspring of creation fit well with the idea of the "creative norm" in Ogyū Sorai's historicism. Both the National Learning and the Ancient Learning Schools argued for a return to a previous ideal age in which an enlightened ruler established order with extraordinary skill and wisdom.

In Satō's work, we can see a syncretic use of both Nativist chauvinism and earlier developments in Confucian political economy. From Nativism, Satō apparently accepted the myths of Japan's divine status and its implications. In his "Confidential Plan of World Unification," (*Kondō Hisaku*), he took Shintō creation myths as a point of departure and reasoned that the Japanese state had the divine mandate to bring order to the rest of the world. This divine mission gave the project of economic development as a prerequisite to ordering the realm a new urgency: "Facing the ocean on four sides, for convenience of ocean transportation it [Japan] has no equal among the nations of the world. Its people, living on sacred land, are superior, excelling those of other countries for bravery and resoluteness."[43] Satō clearly displayed a striking sense of self-confidence in his belief that Japan was well positioned by nature to become one of the world's premier maritime powers.

In light of his understanding of Japan's divine mission to subjugate the world, economics became *developmental* in Satō's mind. That is, rather than the traditional Confucian ideal of political and economic stability, Satō's economics were premised upon change. Innovation of new products and expansion in the production of old ones were crucial components of his economic program. In his *Main Points of Political Economy (Keizai yōryaku)*, for example, Satō added another dimension to the usual definition of "keizai" as "ordering the realm and saving the people." "Keizai is the management of the nation's land, expansion of goods production, promotion of wealth and prosperity in the country, and the salvation of the people. Therefore, the one who rules the country must not neglect this vital work for even one day."[44] In this statement, Satō echoed earlier Confucian political economists in his emphasis on the ruler's obligation to save the people. The ruler must devote his energy to the management of his country's resources at all times to create positive change in the expansion of economic output.

As a matter of concrete policy, Satō advocated a comprehensive state-run industrial system in which every detail of economic life was to be carefully guided by state officials, so "each industry will acquire proficiency and perfect itself, providing steadily increased benefits for the greater wealth and prosperity of the state."[45] Satō's emphasis on state control to increase the domain's production capacity fit in well with what was going on in Satsuma already. Satsuma under Shigehide was more interested in commerce with samurai officials from the central domain bureaucracy increasing their influence over local production. Satō's ideas of further centralization and complete state management would have found a very receptive audience among Satsuma's domain officials. His vision of an all powerful monarch in touch with an original creative norm and actively managing economic change provided a philosophical justification for daimyo to increase their power over the political economy of their domains.

From his Dutch Studies, Satō also had some understanding of international trade. He used England as an example of how Japan might develop its potential as a trading state.

> In the present-day world the country of England is militarily powerful and prosperous, and has control over a very large number of foreign nations, so that the world trembles at its might. This country may be likened to Japan, but the English homelands lie between fifty degrees north, and as a northern land it has a cold climate and its natural products are excelled by our Japanese products. However, because they have successfully sent ships out across the oceans and have traded with the nations of the world they have now become a most powerful and thriving people. Thus we can know that shipping and trade are important tasks for the nation.[46]

In this passage, there is an early version of what the Meiji leaders would call "building the nation through trade" (*bōeki rikkoku*). England's position as an island nation off the coast of a great continent allowed her to build a great empire by exploiting advantages in trade and shipping. With creative leadership, Japan could do the same.

Satō's vision of Japan dominating the nations beyond the sea had wide appeal. His strategy of using trade as the principal means of extending Japan's dominion also caught on among government officials struggling to find solutions to their states' financial difficulties. Finally, his call for an authoritarian state to control every facet of trade development reinforced the samurai class' desire to recapture the power over society that they felt was slipping away as their domains sunk further and further into debt to merchants.

Satō Nobuhiro provided advice to a number of daimyo who were trying to find ways to improve their domains' production to bring in more revenue to their treasuries. Some time in the late 1820s, Satsuma officials solicited his opinion on Satsuma's condition and its prospects for commercial improvement. Satō remembered the encounter as follows: "The following year I went to Edo and took up residence at Nakabashi.

When I wrote *How to Administer Satsuma* [in 1830] on behalf of Igai, the Chief Officer of Satsuma fief, who had enrolled as my student, the Lord of Satsuma was so pleased he sent me an honorarium in the personal care of Yamamoto Rihei and Tanaka Shichibei."[47]

From what we know of Satsuma, it makes sense that its ministers would be most interested in agriculture. The domain state under Shigehide had been nearing the limit in its ability to generate revenue. Igai must have hoped that Satō could provide additional ideas.

Satō's *How to Administer Satsuma (Satsuma Keii ki)* laid out a plan for Satsuma's further development of its resources.[48] The introduction began with the familiar exhortation on the importance of agriculture: "The study of agricultural encouragement and development of products is fundamental to enriching the country and a crucial duty in the salvation of the people."[49] In this way, Satō put his remarks in the context of the *keisei saimin* political economy discourse that would have been familiar to Satsuma officials.

To build up the domain's wealth, Satō proposed the following actions: First, domain bureaucrats should conduct a thorough survey of natural conditions within the domain and make note of any products with potential for development. He argued that crops were dependent upon the domain's latitude and longitude, its climate, and the richness of its soil. Successful domains should consider these variables and specialize in products according to natural conditions. For this reason, he wrote, "Economic administration of a country must begin with a survey of the domain's land."[50]

Once a ruler understood the specific characteristics of the territory, Satō argued, careful attention should be paid to creative forces at work in nature. With a mystical reverence for the sages and deities of the past and the creative spirits of the present, Satō encouraged leaders to work carefully with nature to bring prosperity to the realm.

All of the things people need for daily life springs from the two treasuries. From the two treasuries of land and water all things issue forth without limit. Because these can never be exhausted, they have the honorific title of "Treasuries Without Bounds." However, all things that spring forth from these two treasuries do so according to the heavenly principles of cultivation. When these heavenly principles are not followed, these gifts are not sufficiently granted. This is why the correct path follows the divine will of the ancient sages and creative spirits. To pretend to do the work of agricultural development, one must study this path carefully . . . But if expansion is attempted without observing the way of cultivation, the divine nourishing energy will gradually weaken. The growth of all things will gradually decrease and bring poverty to the country and hunger and cold to the peasants.[51]

Like the land, the territory's people were a resource that needed to be cultivated. As Satō put it, "To invigorate the people, they must first be provided with food, clothing, housing, tools, and capital."[52] Satō recognized that morale was an important element in improving economic production. He built upon Confucian notions of official benevolence and called for state paternalism on the practical grounds of increasing productivity.

Satō also believed that the success of the domain's economic endeavors depended in large measure upon the leaders' moral qualities. Following the Confucian tradition, if the ruler were a sage, all would be well with the people. "Therefore, the essential way is for those on high to relay the creative spirit of the ancient sages."[53] Moral judgment and innovative solutions to problems should become the standard of wise leadership rather than strict adherence to past practices.

For the people to be efficient, state officials would have to educate them in proper methods. Satō suggested that administrators be dispatched to the islands to manage the people more efficiently. "Caretakers should be dispatched to educate the islanders. They are ignorant, if they are taught with directness and kind sincerity, production can be increased three to five fold when they follow instruction."[54] The idea of officials learning advanced techniques and in turn instructing the peasants was one of the main pillars of Satō's plan to increase economic productivity.

Furthermore, the domain had to research new commercial opportunities. Satō noted that the domain was already producing sugar, pottery, and wax. With the application of science, it was possible to create others. He used the term *kyūrigaku* for science. Dutch scholars used this term, which literally meant "study in the mastery of truth," to integrate Western scientific principles into the Confucian lexicon.[55] He called for the development of seventeen minerals, twenty varieties of trees and plants, fifteen types of animals and fish, and fifty-two other miscellaneous items.[56]

If current knowledge was insufficient, Satō urged Satsuma to seek out productive technology in other regions. To illustrate the point, he used the example of the fishing industry:

Your domain faces the Pacific Ocean on three sides. With your warm climate and many islands, you should be recording a gain in your sea products. But, exporting to other lands is *kokueki* and the only product your domain is known for is one type of dried bonito and its value is low. Fishing villages are not abundant. As I said before, this is all due to the islanders' simplistic methods when they have received no instruction. To produce quality goods, it is important to learn from one who is skilled in that product. Now Izu, Sagami, Awa, Kazusa, Shimosa, Hitachi, Ōshū all have fishing villages . . . If your domain adopted their ways, your products would be of the best quality in Japan.[57]

In an early form of conscious technology transfer, domain would seek out skilled laborers in the industry targeted for development and get them to teach their skill to Satsuma people.

Satō Nobuhiro built upon the late Tokugawa period discourse on political economy. Using Japanese creation myths to justify increased central control on a Japan-wide scale, he added to the previous view that the ruler had an obligation to promote economic prosperity in his realm. Satō tempered this lofty vision, however, with extensive research into agricultural and commercial practices throughout Japan. His ideas drew a following among daimyo desperate to build up their economic reserves to solve their financial crises. Satsuma officials had been promoting domain monopolies for some time and found Satō's views on state control hospitable to their own political orientations. These Satsuma officials proved to be ready pupils and, under Zusho Hirosato's leadership, they quickly turned around Satsuma's dismal financial situation.

Conclusion

By the mid-1840s, when Ōkubo Toshimichi and other future Meiji leaders, then in their teens, were entering the domain Zōshikan school, Satsuma's economic ideology had taken a turn in a strategic realist direction. On one hand, it was the "North Pole of conservatism" with Confucian feudal values and practices still very much in control of the people's daily lives. Financial necessity, however, forced the state to use its power to make reforms and improve Satsuma's productive capacity for commercial products. Daimyo Shimazu Shigehide had taken an interest in Western science and had dabbled in its commercial applications, but he was never able to make them generate enough revenue to justify the cost of research. Near the end of his life, he had Satō Nobuhiro write his opinion on how Satsuma could get out of its financial predicament. Satō's main theme was for the state to take firm control, make necessary technological improvements, and increase the quantity and quality of production through active management.

In 1827, Shimazu Shigehide gave Zusho Hirosato the unenviable job of implementing drastic reforms. Zusho proved to be an able administrator and recruited merchants and samurai to implement his reforms. When Westerners began to approach the Ryūkyū Islands, Satsuma was in the financial position to buy Western military technology for its self-strengthening movement. In the 1850s, Shigehide's great grandson Shimazu Nariakira would build upon Zusho's reforms, implement a comprehensive industrial policy, and launch the careers of the future Meiji leaders.

CHAPTER 3

Shimazu Nariakira and Japan's First Industrial Policy

When Satsuma's financial situation deteriorated to the point of crisis, daimyo Shimazu Shigehide appointed Zusho Hirosato (1776–1848) to reform Satsuma's economy. Zusho's reforms incorporated many of the ideas of the realist political economists. Satō Nobuhiro's vision of improving quality through importing better productive technology was particularly influential. In administrative practice, we can see in Zusho's Satsuma administration a proto-developmental state. Officials from the central domain bureaucracy conducted feasibility studies for new products. They directed merchants and peasants into the production of these goods. Skilled workers from other domains were recruited to teach Satsuma peasants new productive and organizational techniques. Capital was allocated to ventures according to the central domain government's plans. At every step of production and distribution, samurai from the central domain bureaucracy were actively involved in management. Zusho's developmental vision closely followed Satō Nobuhiro's blueprint of an authoritarian command economy that made production decisions and allocated resources to maximize revenue for the domain's central treasury.[1]

The need for stable revenue became all the more acute when Satsuma's involvement with the Ryūkyū Islands brought the domain in conflict with the Western powers well before leaders in the rest of Japan had to consider abandoning the seclusion policy. Within Satsuma, the Western threat sparked a power struggle between Zusho's hard line faction that favored continued seclusion and the daimyo's heir Shimazu Nariakira (1809–1858) who acknowledged the need for some concessions to Western demands to buy time for a vigorous self-strengthening program. Nariakira realized that Zusho's unwillingness to cooperate with the bakufu seriously undermined the security not only of Satsuma but also of the rest of Japan. With the bakufu's help, Nariakira eliminated Zusho and forced his own father's retirement. As daimyo, Nariakira instituted a set of visionary reforms to incorporate Western technology into Satsuma's economic strategy. These included an industrial policy to bring Satsuma's economy to a competitive level with the West in both trade and military power.

To formulate his industrial policy, Nariakira built upon earlier developments in Confucian political economy and incorporated insights from Dutch scholars such as Takano Chōei. Takano argued that Japan should actively pursue trade relations with the West to gain wealth, which he saw as the foundation of power. Nariakira vigorously pursued Western learning and research in modern industrial techniques. His ideas had an important influence on his young samurai protégés, who later became key leaders in the Meiji government.

Zusho Hirosato's Authoritarian Approach to Economic Development

By the early nineteenth century, financial problems of the Tokugawa domains were becoming more acute. When a series of bad harvest produced several years of famine during the Tempō period in the 1830s, the domains had to rely even more upon their own resources and direct their attention inward toward their own problems. Shimazu Shigehide realized that drastic reform measures needed to be taken. He appointed his tea master Zusho Hirosato (sometimes referred to as Zusho Shōzaemon) to head the reforms in 1827. To bring in someone from outside the domain's top officials to head domain reforms not only gave them the appearance of real change, but also provided a ready scapegoat if anything went wrong. Zusho's humble status as a tea ceremony attendant perhaps also made him more trustworthy than senior officials might have been by virtue of his dependence on the daimyo's favor for his position.

The Tempō era (1830–1844) is remembered both as a time of trouble and as one of the eras of reform. In 1833, a severe famine hit Japan. The Tōhoku region in northeast Japan was hardest hit, but its effects were felt in other regions. The weather was unusually cold in the spring and summer, which were crucial growing months for rice. The Tōhoku region produced only 35 percent of its normal crop and harvests in the south were poor. The next two years were a little better, but 1836 was much worse.[2] By 1836–1837, people were starving to death in great numbers. Estimates of losses in the Tōhoku region ran at 100,000 people.

The Tokugawa bakufu treasury suffered from declines in production. Its 1.25 million *koku* of revenue in 1833 dropped to 1.03 million *koku* in 1836. By 1837, the price of rice in Osaka had soared to three times what it had been in 1833.[3]

This acute economic situation sparked a marked increase in social disturbances. Mass pilgrimages to the Great Shrine at Ise known as *okage-mairi* had been occurring in 60-year cycles throughout the Tokugawa period. One was expected in 1830, but its scale of five million people over four months caught officials by surprise. Aoki Kōji's research has estimated that there were also 464 rural disputes, 445 peasant uprisings, and 101 urban riots and that these disturbances reached their peak during the famine in 1836.[4]

In the midst of this crisis, the Tokugawa bakufu attempted to reassert its control. Mizuno Tadakuni (1793–1851) became the senior councilor in 1834 and the chairman in 1841. His reforms were generally fundamentalist. He dismissed 1,000 hired officials, issued sumptuary edicts, censored the arts and literature that he considered indecent, forcibly returned peasants found in cities to their farms, ordered new land reclamation, and abolished bakufu sponsored monopolies.[5] Unfortunately for the bakufu, these reforms failed to turn back the tide of social and economic change. Samurai continued to fall further into debt to merchants. Peasants continued to engage in activities for commercial gain. The failure of the reforms also compromised faith in the bakufu's ability to govern.

Satsuma instituted another series of reforms in the Tempō era under Zusho Hirosato. Satsuma was plagued by rising debt during Shimazu Shigehide's tenure as daimyo. By 1827, it had reached the point that the domain could no longer afford to pay the interest. To find a solution to this dilemma, Shigehide put Zusho in charge of reforming the domain's economic policies. Zusho Hirosato had little experience in financial matters, but he proved to be a man of strong will and was successful in turning around the domain's finances.

To address the problem of the domain's debt, Zusho presented its creditors in Osaka with a plan for repayment of the 5,000,000 *ryō* at no interest over 250 years. This amounted to the repudiation of a large debt and it predictably caused quite a stir in the Osaka financial world. Unable to borrow any more money, Satsuma had to follow a strict policy of balanced budgets and self-reliance.[6]

Zusho began by drastically cutting expenses. Most of Shigehide's expensive Dutch Studies projects were cut after his death in 1833. Unnecessary personnel were dismissed from domain service. Funds for keeping up the Satsuma presence in Edo were cut to a minimum. Samurai stipends decreased as new special taxes were levied. Zusho also issued the usual sumptuary decrees against luxury at all levels. None of these measures enhanced Zusho's popularity. Yet with the firm support of the retired daimyo Narinobu and daimyo Narioki, Zusho was able to carry out his plans.

To generate additional revenue, Zusho turned to Satsuma's traditional products and implemented Satō's strategy of (1) finding new products, (2) increasing productive efficiency of traditional production, and (3) improving quality so that Satsuma's goods could command higher prices.

To cultivate new products and expand old ones, Zusho recruited talent from among the merchants. "For example, Sakō Gorōheiei for forestry, Ibusuki no Kuroiwa Fujizaemon for fertilizer, Katō Heihachi for cows, horses, and seaweed, Kirino Sontarō for wax, Yakushi Jinzaemon for sulfur, Hamazaki Taheiji for *konbu* . . . and especially in cotton spinning, Omohisa Jizaemon as head and Kawaida Fujisuke, Nagakura Ihachi, Hitoshi Genzaemon, and Taniyama Jinzaemon, and in silk spinning Kawahata Seizaemon were each recruited."[7]

Zusho also brought in technology from more advanced areas to open these industries. Women skilled in the raising of silkworms came from Ōmi; weavers came from Nishijin; miners came from Miike; and skilled wax tree cultivators came from Matsuzaki in Chikugo.[8] These skilled workers taught the people of Satsuma how to produce new items. Soon Satsuma was producing them both as substitutes for import and for export. This technology transfer policy may well have inspired the Meiji government to invite such large numbers of foreign technicians (*Oyatoi gaikokujin*) to teach modern industrial methods.

Zusho also focused on improving the quality of Satsuma's products. Rice was, of course, the most important commodity. Before the reforms, Satsuma rice had a very low reputation among rice merchants in Osaka. Growing methods were poor and rice was often damaged in shipment. By introducing new varieties of rice and improving cultivation, historian Kanbashi Norimasa has argued, Zusho's administrators were able to improve rice quality to the point that it commanded a much better price in Osaka. During the Bunsei period (1818–1830) the average price for rice was 52.812 *momme* of silver per *koku* of rice. By the end of the Tempō period, this had risen to 96.383 *momme* per *koku*, an 82 percent increase.[9]

Zusho had a similar success with wax. Before his reforms, the wax produced in Satsuma was inferior to the wax from other regions. Zusho had Kirino Sontarō conduct a study of white wax production in central

Japan, Kyoto, and Nagasaki. He also brought back people to teach their skills to peasants already engaged in wax production.[10] After the industry was reorganized and additional productive technology was introduced, Satsuma wax was more valuable. In the Bunsei period, the average price of one *kin* of wax was 1.107 *momme*. By the Tempō period, this was 2.139 *momme* per *kin*.[11]

The same thing occurred in Satsuma' cultivation of rapeseed. Before the reforms, shipments often included dirt and sand with the rapeseed. The reforms brought better methods of harvesting and packaging and the value increased accordingly. The average price rose from 61.28 *momme* per *koku* of rapeseed to 97.986 *momme* per *koku* during the Tempō era. Satsuma medicinal herbs were already selling well in the rest of Japan. Producers had grown careless, however, and had racked up significant debt. Zusho confiscated herb gardens and put new people in charge. He also started trading directly with nearby domains rather than relying exclusively on the Osaka market with some success.[12]

Satsuma monopolized trade with the Ryūkyū Islands to circumvent the bakufu's controls on trade. This helped the domain to bring in needed specie.[13] It also gave Satsuma a corner on Ryūkyū products that could be produced nowhere else in Japan. Satsuma officials also increased production and improved quality of Ryūkyū saffron used as a perfume and a dye. Another Ryūkyū product that Satsuma was able to sell in Japan was cinnamon. It had long enjoyed a good reputation for high quality, but measurement and distribution was difficult. After it left the Ryūkyū Islands it passed through a number of checkpoints before it reached markets in Kyoto and Osaka. At each step, officials would extract a portion of the shipment. After 1838, Satsuma started trading directly with the officially licensed cinnamon guild (*za*) in Edo. This increased the amount of profits that the domain could keep.[14]

The most lucrative venture, by far, was the sugar monopoly that Satsuma already operated. The climate of Satsuma and the Ryūkyū Islands was well suited to producing sugar and had been doing so since 1695. Peasants grew sugar in addition to their subsistence crops. Over time, the domain officials took control of sugar production and reduced the peasants to virtual slavery under samurai managers.[15] Zusho's reforms tightened the domain's grip on sugar production and plugged holes in its monopoly. Anyone caught buying or selling sugar received the death penalty and those pilfering it for private consumption were beaten severely.[16] Zusho also worked to open up new sugar production in other areas of Satsuma including Sakurajima and Tarumizu, Ibusuki, and Ei.[17]

In addition to these draconian measures to increase production, Zusho's officials also worked on improving the quality of the sugar produced for export. They dispatched experts to Ōshima to teach methods of sugar production. Zusho then sent people from Ōshima to other sugar producing areas to teach what they had learned.[18]

Since general price levels throughout Japan rose rapidly during the same period, the actual extent to which improvements in quality contributed to higher prices for Satsuma goods was probably less dramatic than these numbers suggest. Even so, increased production and appreciation in value helped Satsuma improve its revenue considerably.

In spite of his success in turning around the domain's finances, Zusho Hirosato's reforms were generally unpopular. His cutbacks on expenses hit the samurai hardest since they were dependent upon the domain budget for their stipends. His management of the sugar monopoly and other products put even tougher burdens on the people whose labor produced them. Yet, his drastic action put Satsuma in the financial position to innovate in response to domestic and international challenges.

The Western Challenge Comes Early to Satsuma

Western overtures for trade treaties with the Ryūkyū Kingdom came a decade before Commodore Perry's 1853 mission to Japan. Satsuma's interests in the Ryūkyū Islands thrust Shimazu Nariakira to the center of national level politics. Working with the Tokugawa bakufu Abe Masahiro, Nariakira overcame Zusho Hirosato's control over the domain and forced daimyo Shimazu Narioki's retirement. As daimyo, Nariakira replaced Zusho and Narioki's provincialism with a vision of Japan as a whole preparing its economy and military to resist the Western powers.[19]

Shimazu Nariakira was born in 1809; the same year Shigehide purged the writers of the *Kinshiroku* critique of his policies. Nariakira's father Shimazu Narioki was heir to the daimyo of Satsuma. His mother was the daughter of Ikeda Harumichi of the Okayama domain. She was well learned in the Chinese classics and she made sure that Nariakira got a first rate classical education. From the *waka* poems that Nariakira composed as a youth, we also see that Tendai Buddhism was influential in his life and thought. As a samurai, he also received training in the martial arts including gunnery.[20]

In 1812 when Nariakira was four years old, his marriage was arranged with Tokugawa Nariatsu's fourth daughter Fusahime.[21] This family connection with the Hitotsubashi branch of the Tokugawa family would prove important as Nariakira later maintained close contact with Tokugawa Nariaki, daimyo of Mito.

Shimazu Shigehide apparently had a special attachment to his great grandson and Nariakira inherited his interest in Dutch Studies. In 1826, Shigehide and Nariakira accompanied Siebold, the German physician attached to the Dutch trading post at Nagasaki, on his trip to Edo. Like other daimyo heirs, Nariakira grew up in Edo as a hostage in the alternate attendance system. In Edo, he became an accomplished scholar in both the Confucian tradition and Dutch Learning. Nariakira studied Dutch Learning for four years in Edo with Yoshii Shichirozaemon Yasutsugu who was Sugita Genpaku's disciple. To practice European letters, Nariakira kept a diary in Japanese using the Western alphabet.[22]

After the Opium War ended in 1842, the Western powers tried to gain commercial concessions from the Ryūkyū Kingdom. As a Satsuma protectorate, the Ryūkyū Kingdom's crisis forced Satsuma to engage Western demands for trade nearly a decade before the Tokugawa shogumute was confronted with Perry's ultimatum to sign a trade treaty. The British had approached the Ryūkyū Kingdom in search of trading opportunities in 1819 and 1832. In 1824, a British whaling ship precipitated a violent confrontation in which one man was killed when the crew tried to steal cattle and horses. After this incident, the Tokugawa gave an order in 1825 that foreigners were to be driven away "without a second thought."[23]

The French ship *Alcmène* in 1844 made the first serious attempt to negotiate a trade treaty with the Ryūkyū Kingdom. The king's ministers refused to conclude such a treaty and the French withdrew promising to bring a fleet when they returned. The French missionary Théodore Augustin Forcade and his Chinese interpreter were left behind, much to the consternation of local officials, to study the language so they could act as interpreters when the fleet returned.

The fleet returned in 1846 and attempted to negotiate a treaty by force. Although the French officers allowed their men to go ashore and wander freely in Naha, the king remained firm in his rejection of the treaty. In 1847, both French and British warships measured the depth of coastal waters and made maps of the Ryūkyū Islands without permission.[24]

With the escalating Western presence in the Ryūkyū Islands, Satsuma was forced to engage the question of whether or not to open its protectorate to foreign trade. It was clear that the French and British would not go away without some kind of concession. Clearly, extraordinary leadership was required to find a suitable solution to the crisis. As Robert Sakai has shown, the bakufu believed that Shimazu Nariakira was the best leader to handle the Westerners in the Ryūkyū Islands.[25]

Zusho Hirosato was in firm control of Satsuma after Shigehide's death. The daimyo Narioki was a rather weak individual and depended upon Zusho's ability and experience. Unfortunately for the bakufu,

Zusho and Narioki were mainly concerned with maintaining Satsuma's interests. Satsuma had long chafed under the bakufu's restrictions on trade and commerce and its political subjugation of the *tozama* domains. In fact, Zusho and Narioki were delighted to see the bakufu embarrassed in foreign diplomacy so they could build up Satsuma's prestige at the bakufu's expense.

In the summer of 1846, Zusho submitted a report on the growing crisis to Abe Masahiro, the bakufu's chief councilor and met personally with the shogun. He reported that 700 samurai had been dispatched to the islands, but they would be unable to repel a full-scale attack. Zusho, therefore, advocated trade concessions. Such concessions would, of course, bring Satsuma great profit if the domain was allowed to monopolize trade with France. Abe with good reason did not trust Zusho. As it turned out, Zusho lied about the number of samurai, which proved to be only 150, dispatched to confront the French.

After conferring with his advisor on foreign affairs, Tsutsui Masanori, Abe secretly sent Tsutsui to consult with Nariakira. This was an exceptional move since the bakufu traditionally excluded the *tozama* domains from policy deliberations. In his meeting with Tsutsui, Nariakira suggested that allowing the Ryūkyūans to conduct limited trade with the French was preferable to provoking a confrontation for which Japan was ill prepared. He also worried that a hard line response might provoke the French to take the matter up with the Chinese who also claimed suzerainty over the island kingdom and exclude the Japanese altogether.[26]

Nariakira's response reflected a sense that Japan was something larger than the Satsuma domain. Perhaps owing to his Dutch Studies, Nariakira had a wider view of the world than Zusho or Narioki had. Indeed, one of his prized possessions was a globe purchased from the Dutch.[27] From his study of world geography, he apparently realized that Japan's position in the rest of the world transcended narrow domain interests in domestic politics. In Nariakira's mind, the Japanese domains would have to set their differences aside and present a united front to the outside threat. From Nariakira's response to Abe's request for advice, we see the acceleration of several trends until the Meiji Restoration.

First, Nariakira's view indicated an early form of nationalism. Without the Western threat, domains bickered among themselves for power and prestige in the Tokugawa order. The true importance of the Western encroachment on Japanese territory, therefore, was to tilt the political balance away from provincialism toward national unity. Scholars such as Honda Toshiaki and Satō Nobuhiro had been calling for a centralized Japanese state to confront the Western nations, but their appeals for national unity went largely unheard until the foreign threat became real to more people. This threat came first to the Ryūkyū Islands and then to Japan proper. Satsuma's involvement in the Ryūkyū Kingdom's affairs, therefore, brought national consciousness to that domain nearly a decade before the rest of Japan would rally against Perry's "Black Ships."

Nariakira's response also reflected what Japanese scholars have called a policy of "barbarian expulsion via opening the country" (*kaikokuteki jōi*). As this term suggests, Nariakira's policy was a realist solution to the debate between the open country faction and the barbarian expulsion faction within the government. The open country faction called upon the Tokugawa to abandon its anachronistic closed country policy, admit that times had changed, and open Japan to trade with the West. The barbarian expulsion faction took the fundamentalist hard line approach and argued that the Westerners should be repelled by force if necessary. Nariakira's position sought a middle ground. The Western countries clearly had superior armed forces at their disposal and any attempt to resist them by force would be futile. The solution then was to grant as few concessions as possible to avoid an armed confrontation until economic and military preparations could be made. Nariakira's advice indicated an understanding that samurai spirit had to be cultivated. Put another way, Japan's main resource was its people and they needed to be educated to enhance both Japan's military and economic preparedness. This theme of spiritual renewal through training and discipline would be important later in the education of the Meiji leadership.

Finally, Nariakira had a keen strategic mind. He knew very well what the Western powers' next move would be if the Ryūkyū Kingdom failed to come to terms. If the Westerners approached China for concessions, this would compromise Satsuma's (and by extension, Japan's) control over the islands. Clearly, Nariakira had at least a rudimentary understanding of international power politics. Nariakira's proposal made sense to Abe and the bakufu elders, but they had a problem in its implementation. Zusho and the reigning daimyo Narioki were uncooperative. They had lied about the number of samurai dispatched to defend the islands and continued to withhold other important information from the bakufu. Nariakira feared that their behavior would damage relations between Satsuma and the bakufu to the point of compromising national defense.[28]

To ensure that Nariakira's policy proposals would be adopted, Abe Masahiro helped him to get rid of Zusho and force his father Narioki's retirement. Using his friend Lord Date of Uwajima, Nariakira revealed the facts concerning Satsuma's illicit trade with China through the

Ryūkyūs to Abe. When in a meeting with Zusho Abe implied that he knew of what Satsuma had been up to, Zusho took full responsibility for breaking the bakufu's seclusion policy. In late 1848, Zusho committed ritual suicide. Narioki continued in power and Zusho's supporters remained in office for a time. A succession dispute broke out in late 1849 between the supporters of Nariakira, the legitimate heir, and the supporters of Hisamitsu, son of Narioki's favorite consort Yura. When Narioki heard of a plot on the lives of Yura and Hisamitsu, he purged many of Nariakira's supporters, including Ōkubo Toshimichi's father who was sent into exile for four years, and had the leaders commit suicide. Narioki resisted attempts to force his retirement until late 1850 when he was called before the shogun and offered a tea set as a retirement gift. Had he not capitulated and retired, the bakufu was prepared to make public Narioki's complicity with Zusho in the Ryūkyū trade and his failure to make good earlier promises to retire, resulting in disgrace.[29] Nariakira's cooperation with Abe against his father and Zusho marked a new era in Japanese domestic politics. The Western threat forced realignment of factions according to policy rather than domain affiliation. Leaders like Abe Masahiro and Shimazu Nariakira were willing to put aside long-standing antagonism between the bakufu and some *tozama* daimyo in the interest of warding off a common enemy.

It is tempting to draw a stark contrast between Zusho's conservative provincialism and Nariakira's grand vision. This would be unfair, however, because Nariakira's design depended in large measure upon the wealth that Zusho had managed to accumulate. In fact, Zusho's policies remained with Nariakira and later leaders in the form of a concern for the financial base of fiscal expansion. Through much of the early Meiji period, the government would be either unable or unwilling to borrow money abroad and Zusho's ethic of self-reliance served them well. With the transition to Nariakira, the domain's economic policies turned to military concerns. Nariakira became daimyo in 1851 and his programs would place Satsuma in the vanguard of the new discourse on "wealth and strength" (*fukoku kyōhei*) that would evolve through the 1850s and 1860s until the Meiji Restoration. The success of earlier domain monopolies provided the financial foundation to build an expansionist industrial policy. Let us now turn to the sources of Nariakira's ideas.

Takano Chōei's "Open Country" as the Path to Wealth and Power

Takano Chōei's Western scholarship seems to have had considerable influence on Nariakira's thinking. Nariakira mentions Takano in his diary that he kept in the Western alphabet. Several of Takano's books and translations were found in Nariakira's collection.[30] In Takano's writings, we see a pragmatic approach to dealing with the West emphasizing economic growth and military preparedness. Through the lens of late Tokugawa era realist economic thought, Takano saw how the Western countries were pursuing trade to build up their national power. Like other scholars who advocated a policy of wealth and power, Takano advocated opening the country for trade. His style of argument was quite similar to the Confucian scholars', beginning with the assumption that government had a moral responsibility to promote the wealth and strength of the country and people and using historical precedents to show how this moral goal might be accomplished. The main point of difference when compared with traditional Confucian scholars, however, was that these historical examples were drawn not from the Chinese classics, but rather from his study of European history. In this way, Japanese scholars of Dutch Studies, occasionally at a high personal cost, gradually widened the discourse on political economy to seek solutions to problems outside the range of officially acceptable scholarly traditions.

Takano Chōei (1804–1850) was a scholar of Dutch Medicine. He was born in the Sendai domain as the third son of a samurai, but was adopted by his uncle Takano Genzai who was a physician. In 1820, Takano Chōei went to Edo and entered Yoshida Chōshuku's academy of Western medicine. In 1825, he went to Nagasaki to study in Phillip Von Siebold's *Narutakijuku*, an academy of Western learning. Siebold was a German physician who came to Nagasaki as a medical officer for the Dutch trading mission. He was the same doctor whom Shimazu Shigehide and Nariakira had accompanied to Edo in 1826. After five years in Nagasaki, Takano returned to Edo, became a physician, and published Japan's first book on physiology in 1832. He became acquainted with Watanabe Kazan (1793–1841), a famous Edo scholar of Dutch Studies, and studied various fields of Western knowledge.[31]

In June 1837, the American ship *Morrison* sailed into the bay at Edo to return Japanese castaways and to begin trade. In keeping with the shogun's seclusion policy, samurai at Uraga fired at the ship. When they heard about the "Morrison Incident," Watanabe and Takano wrote several papers criticizing the bakufu's actions and advocating a more open policy toward the West. Bakufu officials, of course, were not pleased and in 1839, they arrested Watanabe, Takano, and several of their followers in what became know as the "Imprisonment of the Barbarian Scholars" (*bansha no goku*). Takano was released in 1844, but Watanabe committed suicide in 1841. After his release, Takano traveled to the Uwajima domain and elsewhere translating Dutch books to make his living.[32]

During his sojourn, Takano visited Satsuma under the auspices of Nose Jinshichi who later relayed the story to Ichiki Shirō, the author of the main sources we have on Nariakira. Nariakira trusted Takano and was impressed by his opinions. He asked Takano for copies of his works including "An Aid to Knowing Them" (*Kare wo shiri ichijo*), which we examine in detail below.[33] Because an empirical link between Takano Chōei's writings and Nariakira's thought can be established, it is worth examining Takano's ideas in some detail. His case provides a good example of how scholars of heterodox ideas interacted with enterprising daimyo in the late 1840s and early 1850s to alter the direction of policy debates.

Written as a story of a dream about several prominent scholars gathered to debate recent policy, Takano Chōei's "Tale of Dreams" (*Yume monogatari*) was a thinly veiled critique of the bakufu's handling of the *Morrison* Incident. Misunderstanding "Morrison" as the name of a British official rather than of an American ship, Takano opens the story with one of the scholars asking what kind of country England was. One of the other scholars gathered for the meeting, replied with a rather extensive summary of English geography and history. It was an island to the north of Holland about the same size as Japan. It was a cold country and had a smaller population than Japan. As for its people, the scholar summarized them as follows:

> Their national character is active and inquisitive and they tirelessly investigate various matters. They gladly encourage learning and have as their top priorities research in industrial technology, practice in the military arts, wealth for the people, and strength for the nation.[34]

Then he continued with a discussion of the history of the British Empire. Thanks to geography, England had managed to escape serious damage in the Napoleonic wars. As an island country, England was able to focus on trade and had become rich and powerful. Consequently, the British extended their influence far beyond their shores to North and South America, Africa, India, China, and the islands near Japan.

Takano's scholar elaborated on British activity in China. Canton had become a British trading post with the English getting rich at China's expense, with other European countries following suit. When the Chinese called for an end to the Canton trade, they were powerless to stop it. When asked why the English did not know to turn over Japanese castaways to the Dutch for return to Japan, the scholar demonstrated remarkable understanding of international affairs. The English, he said, had long been interested in establishing trading ties with Japan and used the return of castaways as an excuse. The British, he explained, were trying to circumvent the Dutch monopoly through Nagasaki and trade directly with Edo. They had done the same thing in China by sending gifts directly to the Qing court to get around the local officials in Canton.

Then the scholar was asked how the British would respond when their ship was fired upon under the shogun's seclusion policy. His response was interesting. He said that in Western countries, people value life highest of all. In a recent war between England and Denmark, a British ship sent a message to the shore batteries in Copenhagen that several Danish prisoners were aboard. The Danes then called a cease-fire until their countrymen could be returned. If this was how war was prosecuted in the West, they must consider the Japanese to be without virtue and without principle to fire upon a ship with their own countrymen aboard. The British would interpret this as weakness and it would invite further attack.

Finally, Takano's scholar advocated a policy change. Appropriate harbors at Nagasaki or elsewhere should be designated so that the British could return castaways. The Dutch only provided the news that they wanted the Japanese to hear. If the government adopted a cooperative position toward the British, there was much more that could be learned.

Of course, Takano could not come right out and criticize the bakufu. His scholar in his story said, "I am afraid that I have invited the misunderstanding that I have debated the state's honorable policy. I have done nothing more than respond to the question that you have asked." In spite of his attempts to soften the blow, Takano's *Story of a Dream* stated what many familiar with Western learning must have been thinking. The bakufu's seclusion policy was no longer appropriate to the times. British economic interests already embraced most of East Asia. It was only a matter of time before Japan would be forced to confront Western demands for trade.

Takano's most important work to Nariakira's thinking was "An Aid to Knowing Them" (*Kare wo shiri ichijo*). In this treatise, Takano outlined what the Western nations' strategy was in Asia and how Japan should respond to it. He began by saying that the seclusion policy has worked well and that the people have enjoyed 250 years of peace. He warned, however, that only a wealthy and powerful country could keep the foreigners out since they had come multiple times and would probably keep coming in search of trade.

Again, Takano used China's example. When the Chinese had prohibited the sale of opium, the English attacked, extracting an indemnity and forcing open five ports. Other Western powers jumped aboard and began trade with China. In the Ryūkyū Islands, England and France pursued trading rights by force. The Qing Dynasty in China was weak and the Western countries had many powerful ships with accurate weapons. It would be difficult to defend Japan against them. If the Westerners occupied the Ryūkyū Islands, it would be a great hazard to the main islands of Japan. Preparations would have to be made.

From this summary of the first section, it is clear that Takano had a realist perspective on the foreign question. He does not spend much time debating the merits of the seclusion policy. He merely states, using China's misfortune as an example, the fact that under current circumstances Japan could not mount successful military resistance against the Western powers.

To find a solution to Japan's dilemma, Takano turned to an in-depth analysis of the origin of British and French power in a subsection he entitled, "Origins of Western aggression in foreign lands, methods of building a wealthy country and powerful military through trade, and profits from trade."[35] Takano began this section with a discussion of Western expansion since Columbus. He discussed the Spanish and Portuguese expansion of trade with India and the Americas and their conquests. America, he said, was originally inhabited by uncivilized savages much like Japan's Ainu. With their bows and arrows, these people were no match for Western firearms.

Through trade and conquest, the Europeans became wealthy and powerful. Takano summarized the British and Dutch cases as follows:

> Although they were originally barren and rocky, England and Holland as island and coastal countries were well positioned to sail the seas. Through trade they became rich and powerful countries. Their conditions long ago and now are completely different. Their material wealth is in direct opposition to the natural conditions of their lands. This is related to the diligent effort of their people.[36]

This theme would become very important in later Japanese thinking on political economy. The Europeans had become powerful over time. The natural order had nothing to do with it. Rather, human effort exploited what little advantage nature offered and built empires. For the shrewd leaders, overseas trade offered an opportunity for expansion of the country's wealth and power.

Takano continued with a detailed analysis of British and French military potential. This included statistics on the number of ships, troops, and weapons that each country had deployed in India and Asia. He also detailed the goods that each nation produced and how much profit they made from trade. From Takano Chōei's work, we can see a distinctly samurai perspective. He evaluated countries and cultures according to their military power. Trade produced wealth and wealth created power. In this sense, conditions in the outside world were interpreted through the economic nationalist framework. Since the domains in Japan had been trying to trade to improve their wealth and stature in the Tokugawa system, Western behavior was readily comprehensible. States pursued their interests without regard for moral sensibilities. If the Japanese wished to maintain their territorial integrity, they would have to take economic realist thinking to the national level.

Takano Chōei was an example of a thinker that brought the realist streams of Confucian political economy and Dutch Learning thinking together. Takano and other scholars appropriated the term *fukoku kyōhei* (rich nation and strong military) from the ancient Chinese Legalist ideas of Guan Zhong, Lord Shang, and Han Feizi, but emphasized the importance of trade in addition to agriculture as the source of Japan's national power.[37] They justified the revolutionary overturn of the traditional seclusion policy in terms of the tenets of traditional political discourse that appealed to realist leaders. Since Nariakira was interested in both economic development and strengthening his domain against the Western encroachment in Okinawa, it is easy to see why Takano's reasoning appealed to him.

Shimazu Nariakira's Industrial Policy

When Shimazu Nariakira became daimyo in 1851, he immediately began to improve Satsuma's trade and defenses. Building upon Takano Chōei's ideas, Nariakira investigated how Western technology could promote Satsuma's economic development and improve military preparedness. If England and Holland could become world powers with their limited resources, Satsuma could do the same. The key was in effort and the pursuit of technical knowledge.

His policies included both import substitution and export promotion strategies. Although he was primarily concerned with military defense, he was keenly aware of the importance of economic strength. Economic development and military considerations were closely related in Nariakira's mind. In fact, Nariakira conducted a form of industrial policy that foreshadowed the Meiji campaigns for wealth and power.

Nariakira's victory over the Zusho–Narioki faction turned Satsuma policy toward fiscal expansionism. Where Zusho was concerned mainly with the accumulation of specie, Nariakira was more willing to invest large sums in risky ventures with the potential for future gains.

Satsuma was, of course, principally an agricultural domain and leaders had to find ways to make agriculture more profitable. Nariakira recognized the importance of agricultural development when he said, "The foundation of political economy (*keizai*) is the promotion of agriculture. As the base of man's livelihood, agricultural promotion is the foundation of administrative action."[38] If agriculture did not prosper, there would not be any funds available for industrial expansion. For this reason Nariakira continued Zusho's promotion of agricultural products as well as traditional industries such as salt, silkworms, fishing, mining, and white sugar.[39] As Satō Nobuhiro recommended many years earlier, Nariakira continued Zusho's policy of importing technical knowledge from outside the domain to promote efficient production. Nariakira, however, did not stop with knowledge from other domains. He also looked into practical applications of Western technology.[40]

Import substitution was an important element in Nariakira's strategy. Substituting domestic manufactures for imported goods advanced several of Nariakira's goals. First, this policy reduced Satsuma's dependence upon imported goods and improved the domain's self-sufficiency. In times of conflict, Satsuma could not depend upon other domains to meet its needs. Second, import substitution improved the balance of trade. Every item that Satsuma people could produce for themselves was something upon which the domain did not need to spend its precious hard currency. Third, through learning to make for themselves more sophisticated goods, the people of Satsuma gained important technical skills. As the skill level of the domain increased, other industries would also develop.

Realizing that agriculture was the main resource his domain had, Nariakira's first concern was to establish an office to improve agricultural technology. As Robert Sakai observed, "He instructed officials in 1854 that samples should be gathered from all over the world so that the best could be made in Satsuma. It was disgraceful, he said, that Satsuma should be importing tools from other *han* at high prices, and particularly when the products were often inferior."[41] By taking the best products available as models, Nariakira urged his people to strive for excellence and engage in an early form of catch-up industrialization. By focusing on quality, Satsuma artisans could provide their own domain with excellent products and have a competitive advantage over other domains that produced shoddy goods.

With the Western presence in the Ryūkyū Islands, Nariakira was of course concerned with improving weapons technology. In 1856, Nariakira noted,

> At this time when defense against the foreign barbarians is of crucial importance it is the urgent duty of all samurai both high and low to cooperate in learning of conditions in foreign lands so that we may adapt their good points to supplement our deficiencies, reinforce the military might of our nation and keep the barbarian nations under control.[42]

Nariakira began by requesting that the bakufu remove restrictions on ship size and allow him to build Western style ships for the defense of the Ryūkyū Islands. Abe Masahiro was supportive of Nariakira and he was therefore given permission to go ahead. A fisherman named Manjirō assisted in the construction of these ships. After he was shipwrecked, he spent eleven years in the United States and became a skilled sailor. When he returned to Okinawa in 1851, he was transported to Kagoshima for forty-eight days of interrogation. Nariakira took a personal interest in the interrogation and Manjirō's knowledge of ships and navigation. In 1854, Satsuma officials examined a Dutch warship in Nagasaki and spent four months with Dutch officers who instructed them in naval technology.[43]

Nariakira had a small industrial complex built on the shore of Kagoshima bay in 1852. A blast furnace was installed in 1854 that produced cannon, cannonballs, and later rifles, glass, and pottery.[44] He also established the Kaibutsukan to translate foreign texts. The Shūseikan was a factory employing 1,300 people that experimented with metallurgy, small arms, ships, drugs, telegraphy, chemical products, glass, and photography.[45]

Nariakira also commissioned translations of Dutch books on steamships, steam engines, telegraphy, gas lighting, and photography. These translators joined a science institute that they established for the construction of these devices in Kagoshima.[46]

Next Nariakira tried to follow the lead of the Saga domain that had built a reverbatory steel furnace in 1848. The first attempt failed, but Nariakira was not deterred. He told his men, "Westerners are people; the men of Saga are people; and Satsuma men are also people. Do not be discouraged. Redouble your research."[47] The second and third attempts also failed, but in 1856 Satsuma succeeded in constructing a working furnace. With it, the domain was able to cast artillery pieces. Nariakira also had his officials study and construct machinery for drilling the bore of cannon. The Satsuma domain faced formidable obstacles when importing Western technology. They had to rely on books and use trial and error methods. Nariakira's optimism and perseverance were inspiring to the young samurai that would later lead the nation.

Although his paramount concern was the defense of his domain, Nariakira also saw the opportunity for economic profit in the arms industry. As Robert Sakai observed,

> While inspecting his industrial projects in 1857, Nariakira declared to his officials that these steel works first would produce some three thousand guns needed for the *han*. Thereafter guns would be sold to other daimyo and to other countries such as China, for he foresaw that in a few years there would be trouble erupting within Japan as well as outside the country. Thus Satsuma's arsenal would not only be essential, but also profitable. Similarly he believed there would be a good market for ships constructed in Satsuma, as indicated already by an order placed by the Bakufu.[48]

Weapons manufacture was a growth industry in East Asia and Nariakira hoped that Satsuma could profit economically. First he concentrated upon substituting Satsuma produced weapons for Western imports. Later he hoped to produce a surplus and send them to other domains for profit.

Perhaps more important than his experiments with Western technology were Nariakira's attempts to reform Satsuma's education system and promote talented samurai beyond what their hereditary ranks would have allowed. Tokugawa ideologues had long lamented the tendency of domains to ignore merit and promote samurai to important office on the basis of their hereditary rank.[49] Nariakira, at least in part, attempted to address this issue by promoting talented men. He dispatched students to Nagasaki, Chōshū, Edo, and Osaka to learn the latest military sciences. He also dispatched teachers to teach gatherings of samurai at the local district level.[50] In addition to incorporating Dutch Studies into the domain school curriculum, he allowed the open study of Wang Yangming Confucianism, which was considered subversive in most domains. Followers of Wang Yangming's approach included reformers such as Yoshida Shōin and Ōshio Heihachirō. This school rejected textual authority and promoted self-cultivation and action.[51]

Nariakira gathered young samurai and trained them himself for several hours each afternoon. Matsukata Masayoshi (1835–1924), who later became one of the Meiji government's leading economic policy makers, was one of these young samurai who benefited from Nariakira's patronage and adopted his views of economic policy.[52] Matsukata was born in 1835 to a lower ranking samurai in Kagoshima. At age thirteen, he entered the Zōshikan domain school that daimyo Shigehide had established in 1773. In 1850, Matsukata assumed a post in the domain treasury for which he received a special award of 130 ryō in 1857. After the Meiji Restoration, Matsukata would become an official in the Ministries of Finance and Home Affairs and in 1881, he would become Minister of Finance and the architect of Japan's banking and financial system.

In fact, most of the Meiji leaders from Satsuma were part of Nariakira's progressive faction. Both Saigō Takamori (1827–1877) and Ōkubo Toshimichi (1830–1878), who together with Kido Kōin (1833–1877) from Chōshū comprised the "triumvirate" of the Meiji Restoration, owed their careers to Nariakira.[53] Nariakira employed Saigō as his personal assistant to keep him close by as an informal adviser. Nariakira made Ōkubo *kura yaku*, an official in charge of receiving grain tribute from Satsuma provinces. Both Saigō and Ōkubo were deeply influenced by Nariakira's views on economic development to strengthen the domain.

Godai Tomoatsu (1835–1885), who became an important business leader in Osaka after the Meiji Restoration, was also a samurai in the Nariakira faction. Godai's father was a Confucian scholar, city magistrate, and was considered one of Nariakira's "brain trust."[54] In 1857, Satsuma sent Godai Tomoatsu to Nagasaki to study gunnery, Dutch, and mathematics at the bakufu's newly established naval school. There he met Katsu Kaishū (1823–1899), a bakufu official with loyalist sympathies who helped arrange the surrender of Edo castle to Saigō's Satsuma forces in the Meiji Restoration.

By giving samurai a chance to prove themselves on the basis of their abilities rather than rank, Nariakira provided an incentive for innovation and creativity. With the new demands that the Western challenge presented, old customs were no longer appropriate. The domain government had to develop new institutions that would encourage new modes of thought rather than blind adherence to tradition.

Conclusion

Shimazu Nariakira was clearly a leader of great vision. He was able to look beyond his domain's interest and see Japan as a whole operating in the world system. He cooperated with the bakufu to present a united front against Western encroachment in Okinawa. With astute judgment, he advocated a realistic policy of granting limited concessions while Japan prepared for confrontation. Under Nariakira's direction, Satsuma took the lead in economic development and military self-strengthening. In this context, a clearly recognizable industrial policy emerged. With the threat from outside, there was an incentive to spend funds on developing self-sufficiency through import substituting industries. The crisis also loosened the hold of tradition and allowed talented young Samurai to rise above their hereditary social status. Most importantly, he instilled in his followers a vision of what could be achieved through diligent effort and serious study.

CHAPTER 4

Confucian and Capitalist Values in Conflict

In the decade before the Meiji Restoration, conflicts with the Western powers intensified the shift in economic ideology toward strategic realism. At first, intellectuals and policy makers hoped that simply importing Western military technology would be sufficient to defend Japanese independence. However, some soon realized that Western military strength was inseparable from the political, economic, and social institutions that supported it. Advocates of more drastic reforms rallied around the slogan "rich country, strong military" (*fukoku kyōhei*) to justify their proposals in the name of national defense.

In Satsuma, even the hard line conservatives, who returned to power after Nariakira's death in 1858, had to admit the need for reform following a disastrous military engagement with the British. To investigate the source of British power, the domain dispatched, in defiance of the bakufu policy, a clandestine mission to Europe. From the mission's report, it became clear to some forward thinking samurai that Western economic institutions may be just as valuable as scientific discovery in the pursuit of national wealth and power.

Japanese Spirit and Western Technology

To meet the foreign threat, thinkers again worked to adjust the existing Confucian ideological framework. Sakuma Shōzan (1811–1864) was one of the most famous intellectuals seeking to reconcile Western technology and Japanese values. He drew from the Zhu Xi's Confucian interpretation of the Way of Heaven as natural principle akin to Western ideas of natural law. If nature's principles were apparent to all, it was possible that Western science outpaced Chinese learning in their discovery. He tried to divorce Western scientific inquiry from morality and assert that Eastern ethics could be asserted while pursuing Western science.

Sakuma grew up as a samurai and was educated in the Confucian tradition in the Matsushiro domain in the mountainous region of central Honshu. In 1833, he left for Edo where he studied Chinese composition with the well-known bakufu scholar Satō Issai. After China's defeat in the Opium War, however, Sakuma turned his attention to Western technology. In 1842, he enrolled as a student in Egawa Tarōzaemon's academy in Edo to study naval defense. Later he studied Dutch and began to read Western texts himself.[1] To accommodate this new knowledge within his Confucian philosophy and values, Sakuma coined the term "Eastern ethics and Western science."

In an 1854 letter Sakuma wrote,

> Nowadays, equipped with Chinese learning alone, one cannot help putting on empty airs. On the other hand, after studying Western learning one may do so great a work as to astound others, yet that work falls short of the sages' deeds. For the study of ethics and human relationships (dōtoku giri) is unknown to Western learning. Therefore, neither Chinese learning nor Western learning alone is perfect unless the two are combined.[2]

Sakuma was probing the frontiers of his traditional ideology trying to find an accommodation with the new learning he encountered. He saw no conflict between his concept of an ethical civilization and Western science. If there was one universal principle, the way of the sages and Western technical skills must be derived from one and the same thing.[3] The great Way simply manifested itself differently according to different historical circumstances. Both Confucian values and Western science were necessary for Japan's future progress.

Sakuma's views on learning were also profoundly practical. In his 1854 Seikenron ("Reflections on My Errors"), which he developed while in a bakufu prison from April to September 1854 for supporting Yoshida Shōin's attempt to stowaway on one of Perry's ships, he wrote,

> Learning, the possession of which is no assistance and the lack of which is of no harm, is useless learning. Useful learning, on the other hand, is as indispensable to the meeting of human needs as are the production of the light hemp-woven garment of summer and the heavy outer clothing of winter.[4]

Learning, whether philosophical or technical, had to serve some purpose. It was not enough to simply know the facts or be able to recite the classics. The important issue for Sakuma and others struggling with how to reconcile Confucian and Western learning was how to apply knowledge to solve problems that people encountered in government and their daily lives.

Western imperialism challenged Confucian moral principle and created an intellectual environment preoccupied with the sources of military power. In this environment, the martial realist elements of samurai tradition soon eclipsed Confucian moral principles. The subjugation of learning to military ends can be seen clearly by examining, again, his 1854 *Seikenron*:

> In order to master the barbarians, there is nothing so effective as to ascertain in the beginning conditions among them. To do this, there is no better first step than to be familiar with barbarian tongues. Thus, learning a barbarian language is not only the first step toward knowing the barbarians, but also the groundwork for mastering them.[5]

One is immediately struck by the amazing confidence and optimism displayed in this text. Mastery of the "barbarians" was never in question in Sakuma's mind. It was simply a matter of finding out exactly what the nature of the Western challenge was and acting decisively to meet this challenge. Here again we see the themes of "ascertaining conditions" among the Western nations and taking appropriate action. Learning Western languages was the foundation for a deeper understanding of the problems facing Japan and a step toward the ultimate goal of mastery of the barbarians. Here Sakuma built upon earlier scholars' historicism. The themes of knowing the actual conditions and taking appropriate action would become guiding concepts for the Meiji leaders.

In economic matters, Sakuma similarly presented trade as the means to military ends. In an 1862 critique of the bakufu policy regarding treaties with the Western powers, Sakuma wrote

> I have not studied finance, but I do know that the various Western countries support their nations with profits from trade. It is with that knowledge that I humbly state my views. In contrast with the current accounting system, a budget plan should be set up using Western accounting methods and a minister selected from the council of elders to see to it that only trade within the framework of the plan is transported in bakufu owned ships. By expanding trade, first with the Qing court in China and then with the whole world, I believe, profits could be used to build up naval defenses and pay the expense of dispatching emissaries abroad.[6]

Sakuma reached the same conclusion Shimazu Nariakira had in Satsuma a decade earlier and advocated the formulation of an economic plan on a national scale. By strategically controlling access to its ships, the bakufu could implement an economic plan.

Later in the same document, Sakuma elaborated his argument:

> We should labor to apply our talents to the study of energy and mechanics and to the work of building useful devices used in foreign lands, providing technical leadership by erecting factories in every province, and exploring the science of production and development of resources. If, with the wealth generated, we could obtain ships and trade with the whole world, profits would expand providing plenty for the expenses of naval defense. If the shogun's ministers were to use any surplus to promote national power, they would come closer year by year to realizing their goal of making Japan the most powerful country in the world.[7]

Here Sakuma called for the importation and diffusion of Western technology to produce goods for trade with the Western nations. The gains from this trade could then be used to promote Japan's national military power.

For Sakuma, then, the key to facing the West on its own terms was power rather than virtue. This was a departure from the Confucian ideal that Mencius had promoted in his praise of the ideal king, who ruled by moral example, and his condemnation of the dictator, who ruled solely by power.[8] Sakuma supported his position with reference to another Confucian classic, the *Shu Jing* (Classic of Documents) in an 1854 letter to a friend:

> It is said that if states are equal in strength their virtue is weighed, and if their virtue is found equal their righteousness is weighed. I believe it is very significant that the word "strength" is placed first. Even a sage could not reign over all states as the ruler of the entire country if he did not command strength sufficient to subjugate them. It is also said in praise of King Wen of [Zhou] that the large states feared his military strength while the small states became attached to his virtue. Therefore, at present, I talk only about strength.[9]

Here Sakuma echoed a by now familiar argument that power was a prerequisite for establishing a moral order. As Sakuma's biographer Richard Chang observed, "By quoting the *Shu Jing*, Shōzan gave Confucian respectability to his un-Confucian conviction that what counted in coping with the West was strength not virtue."[10]

This was a crucial point for Sakuma who was suggesting that Japanese states should reorder their priorities to focus first on power and then on its virtuous use. In earlier *keisei saimin* debates on the moral duty of a ruler to "order the realm and save the people" and policies to develop commerce to enhance the domains' interests (*kokueki*), commerce was begrudgingly accepted as the means to moral ends. With the arrival of the Western threat, attention rapidly turned to military power and any means necessary to obtain it became morally acceptable. Sakuma Shōzan tried to heal the breach between virtue and economic practicality by placing the pursuit of commercial wealth into the lexicon of traditional values, but this would prove exceedingly difficult.

By 1860, many thinkers agreed that Japan would have to adopt Western productive, organizational, and military technologies to protect Japan's sovereignty. The problem was how to draw the line between ethics and science when Western technology required Japanese political, economic, and social reorganization. The leaders of the Meiji Restoration movement solved this problem by elevating the state's wealth and power to the status of prerequisite for all other virtues. From the realist perspective, if the state failed to maintain Japan's independence, any discussion of moral government would be useless. Once the state's wealth and power had been achieved, then the question of what to do with this power could be addressed.

Yokoi Shōnan (1809–1869) became one of the most systematic proponents of this intensified emphasis on state wealth and power. His writings helped popularize the slogan "rich country, strong military" (*fukoku kyōhei*), drawn from histories of the classical Chinese Spring and Autumn and Warring States eras (722–221 BC), that would later guide the Meiji oligarchy in its early years. Yokoi was the younger son of a middle-ranking samurai from the Kumamoto domain in Kyushu. He was educated in the domain school and was selected to study in Edo. At Edo, he came under the influence of Ogyū Sorai's Ancient Learning School and the emerging nationalism of the Mito School. In 1840, he fell out of favor with the Kumamoto domain leadership and became an independent teacher and scholar. He became well respected and advised daimyo on economic and social issues in Fukui and Echizen domains.[11] Like promoters of practical political economy elsewhere, Yokoi advised daimyo to adopt policies to exploit commercial opportunities. Then they could manage the flow of currency to prevent economic stagnation and build their domains' financial strength.[12]

After Commodore Perry's American warships demanding a trade treaty challenged the bakufu's seclusion policy in 1853, Yokoi became one of the leading proponents of *fukoku kyōhei* that would become one of the most enduring slogans of the Restoration government. Yokoi's *fukoku kyōhei* ideas held that Japan should become a first rate world power, but differed from the bakufu's blind wandering, and Sakuma's belligerent strategy. He wanted to cooperate with the Americans to reach a peaceful settlement.[13]

Philosophically, Yokoi differentiated principle (*ri*) and conditions (*sei*). Principle enabled men to grasp reality in times of change to take appropriate action. The early sage kings Yao and Shun erected a political order that was appropriate to a particular place in history.[14] In this line of reasoning, Yokoi followed the same historicist logic that Ogyū Sorai and Dazai Shundai had used. Yokoi also shared with Sakuma Shōzan the belief that the Japanese could somehow keep their core values while adopting Western methods.

In a letter to a friend in Echizen domain in 1859, Yokoi demonstrated that the true measure of the "Way" was in its results:

> The Way is found through heaven and earth. It is not something possessed either by us or by foreigners. Wherever the Way is possessed there you will find the central kingdom even among barbarians; where there is an absence of the Way, there you will find barbarians, even though they are the Chinese or the Japanese.[15]

This clearly opened the way to a pragmatic approach to ethics defining the "Way" as that which would deliver success and power in the international environment. In 1860, Yokoi elaborated this point in his most famous treatise *Kokuze sanron* (Three Principles of National Policy). As the title suggests, he divided the work into three parts, "*Fukokuron*" (The Principle of a Wealthy State), "*Kyōheiron*" (The Principle of a Strong Military), and "*Shidō*" (The Way of the Warrior).

In his section on a state's wealth, Yokoi argued that resisting the world capitalist system was futile:

> Nowadays, on the earth, the various nations are crossing the seas and freely trading with one another. In the midst of this, if Japan were the only one to maintain a closed country policy, it would certainly invite a military attack. As we have seen, Japan already has plenty of trouble even without a war. It is impossible, in the midst of these difficulties, to fortify defenses and assemble samurai to sufficiently repel an invading army or like expelling the barbarians. What a mess! This is the legacy of the closed country policy.[16]

To solve this problem Yokoi advocated surrendering to the inevitable opening of Japan to trade. As Yokoi put it, the trend of the times favored trade:

> If we ride the trend of heaven and earth, according to the situation found in all the nations of the world and govern the realm according to the "Way of common interest" (*kōkyō no michi*), current worries would be solved and all the injuries [of the closed country policy] would be erased.[17]

Yokoi then clearly blamed much of Japan's political and financial distress on the bakufu's foolish attempt to resist world trends. He ended his section on a state's wealth with a warning from China's experience. The Chinese had once been a great empire, but were now humbled by the British, once considered barbarians.

> Although China remains an independent national polity according to England's good will, it must be said that its glory as a great empire has come to naught. China and Japan are as close as one's lips and teeth. If China falls, Japan will follow close behind sharing the same fate. [Without the lips], how cold it will be for the teeth! This is no time to sit back and casually observe. We must follow heaven's virtue, grasp the sages' teaching, know current conditions in all nations, labor to correct our political problems, and produce the results of a rich country and strong military so we will not be despised by the foreign nations.[18]

Confucian morality had not been able to save China from Western aggression, so Yokoi emphasized military concerns in his approach to economic policy. Countries did not pursue wealth for its own sake. Rather, wealth produced power and prestige in the international environment. Japan had to become wealthy and therefore powerful so it would not suffer disgrace at the hands of her enemies. The wise ruler, therefore, followed the sages' example and enacted policies that were appropriate to their historical circumstances.

In his next section, Yokoi addressed the issue of a powerful military (*kyōhei*). Although *fukoku kyōhei* has often been translated as "rich country, strong army" in English, it is important note that *kyōhei* meant naval power to Yokoi and to the early Meiji leaders. Japan was an island nation and the Western threat manifested itself most vividly as foreign ships anchored in its harbors.

Yokoi stated this point clearly, "First of all in the world order (*sekai no keisei*), a navy is of vital importance if one is to profit in maritime ventures." In response to the question of how Japan should build up its power, Yokoi advocated economic development using England as a model:

> Japan is a group of islands in the Eastern Sea off the coast of the Asian states. This is much like England's position in relation to the European states . . . If we look at Japan's situation, a land army is of no use. Rather, it is clear that a navy must be developed quickly. Look at England, for example. England had to raise its military forces and expand its national power to avoid foreign threats and govern its colonies.

At this point, Yokoi listed the number of various types of British warships and concluded;

> Conditions in Japan and England are quite similar so to enact a military strengthening policy that even England cannot defeat. To counter England's warships, we will need to prepare 420 ships, 15,000 large guns, 29,500 sailors, and 13,500 additional combat personnel.[19]

Yokoi concluded his treatise with a discussion of the type of manpower that his reform agenda would require. The "Way of the Warrior" would provide the spiritual fortitude that the Japanese would need to confront Western economic and military aggression. In the section he called "*Shidō*" (The Way of the Warrior), Yokoi wrote,

> To govern the realm, in everyday and crisis moments, a ruler must have talented people. To educate those people, there are only two paths, the way of the warrior and the way of the scholar. I know that the sages of old as well as people today have all educated their personnel in the way of letters and martial arts. However, people today do not understand that this training is also of the heart and mind (*kokoro*). So trying to train talent in today's methods of education, is like steaming sand and trying to eat it as rice.[20]

Yokoi believed that there was more to education than simply the memorization of texts and techniques. Men had to integrate their learning into something larger than themselves. Their task thus became a spiritual mission rather than simply a material exercise.

Yokoi was influential on the young leaders of the Meiji government. Iwakura Tomomi called him to Kyoto to advise the new government.[21] Yokoi addressed the frustration that the younger samurai felt as their educations failed to prepare them for the Western challenge to Japan's traditional order. He also offered some practical suggestions for building up Japan's naval defenses and promoting the economic activity needed to pay for it.

Yokoi was assassinated in 1869 by xenophobic extremists who believed that he supported republican government and might be a Christian. Nevertheless, his economic ideas lived on through Yuri Kimimasa who was the author of the Meiji government's first currency policy. Yuri had been Yokoi's student when he advised the daimyo of the Fukui domain. His proposal of 1868 called for the new government to continue gold-backed paper currency that domains had issued to increase the money supply. He hoped that the increase in available credit would allow local governments to promote industrial projects. In his proposal, Yūri wrote, "The gold notes that the domains issue will become the foundations for national prosperity (*fukoku*). With these [funds], production would be revived and promoted and national profit (*kokueki*) would be increased."[22] Following Yokoi, Yuri also equated mercantile wealth and the national interest.

Sakuma Shōzan and Yokoi Shōnan are two examples of thinkers who responded to the bakufu's foreign affairs misfortunes with renewed emphasis on commercial wealth as the source of state power. There was wide agreement that Japan's current political, economic, and cultural institutions were no longer adequate to address both the economic and military challenge that the Western powers posed. The problem now was just how much adjustment would be necessary.

As the Japanese felt the full implications of their semicolonial status under the treaties, however, discontent with bakufu policy mounted. Opinion among the politically active samurai polarized in the early 1860s around the extreme views of completely "expelling the barbarians" (*jōi*) on one hand and completely opening the country (*kaikoku*) on the other. Sakuma's vision of a reconciliation of Japanese spirit and Western technology faded and, in 1864, radicals assassinated him for being too soft on the issue of barbarian expulsion. Ironically, the assassination of prominent Japanese leaders and foreigners and subsequent Western reprisals forced leaders of the Restoration movement to move even further toward opening the country. As the full power of Western military and industrial technology became more widely apparent, Yokoi's vision of a complete renovation of Japanese society seemed to many leaders of the Restoration as the only alternative.

British Attack and the Satsuma Mission to Europe

In Satsuma, Shimazu Nariakira had pioneered many of the reforms that Sakuma and Yokoi advocated. Nariakira's death in 1858, however, slowed the pace of reform. Despite the conservatives' return to power, the young men whom Nariakira trained remained true to his reform vision. British warships shattered the conservatives' complacency when they exacted revenge for the murder of an Englishman by shelling Satsuma's capital at Kagoshima. This dramatic action tipped the balance once and for all in favor of realist reformers.

After being forced to sign humiliating trade treaties with the Western powers, the bakufu made modest efforts to train their people in Western technology. The bakufu established the Bansho Shirabesho (Office for the Investigation of Barbarian books) in Edo's Kanda district in 1856. The office had a staff of fifteen including three direct retainers of the shogun and three from *tozama* domains of Satsuma, Chōshū and Uwajima and was renamed the Kaiseisho (development institute) in 1863.[23] The bakufu also asked the Dutch to establish a school to train samurai in the naval science in Nagasaki. The Nagasaki Kaigun Denshūsho (Nagasaki Naval Training Academy) was established in 1855. Dutch officers instructed the Japanese in naval technology, maritime transport, gunnery, and shipbuilding.[24] In February 1857, the Satsuma daimyo Shimazu Nariakira sent Godai Tomoatsu (1835–1885) and other Satsuma samurai to study naval science and gunnery at the Nagasaki Naval Training Academy. Godai was the son of a city magistrate who became Nariakira's trusted advisor. When Godai was fourteen years old, Nariakira put Godai's father in charge of trade with the Ryūkyūs. There is a story that Godai's father showed him a map of the world that he had received from the daimyo. When Godai saw that Japan was not even on it, he is reported to have vowed to put Satsuma and Japan on the map suggesting nationalist sentiment from an early age.[25] Godai's time in Nagasaki was important because it exposed him to information from the outside world and helped him make contacts with men from other domains.[26] There he met future leaders in the Restoration including Gōtō Shōjirō, Iwasaki Yatarō, Sakamoto Ryōma, Ōkuma Shigenobu, and Mutsu Munemitsu.[27]

Unfortunately for the Satsuma progressives, Nariakira died suddenly in July 1858 and Nariakira's father Narioki was again in charge as regent for the new daimyo Tadayoshi. Without a son of his own, Nariakira had designated his half-brother Hisamitsu's son Tadayoshi as his heir. Godai was called home in October. Ōkubo Toshimichi, Saigō Takamori, Matsukata Masayoshi, and other progressives also suffered setbacks as conservatives swept them out of office and abandoned Nariakira's ambitious self-strengthening programs including naval defense.

This conservative resurgence in Satsuma did not last long. On July 29, 1858 the shogunate signed the Treaty of Amity and Commerce Between

Japan and the United States, which the American Consul Townsend Harris negotiated. In this treaty, the bakufu agreed to open additional ports to the West at Edo, Kobe, Nagasaki, Niigata, and Yokohama. The treaty also fixed low import duties and established the system of extraterritoriality. This treaty was clearly an egregious affront to Japanese sovereignty and resulted in dissatisfaction with the bakufu. Even the conservatives in Satsuma had to acknowledge the need for a renewed self-strengthening program. In May 1859, Satsuma officials again ordered Godai to Nagasaki where British, American, French, Dutch, and Russian merchants were trading according to their treaties with the bakufu. In September 1859, a Scottish merchant named Thomas Glover established a trading company in Nagasaki. Glover would later assist both Godai and Matsukata Masayoshi in their importation of Western ships and naval technology to Satsuma.

After Narioki's death in 1859, Shimazu Hisamitsu became regent for the young daimyo Tadayoshi and began to restore the progressives whom Nariakira had patronized. He reinstated Ōkubo Toshimichi, who had been purged in the conservative backlash after Nariakira's death. In March 1860, Ōkubo, thanks to Hisamitsu's favor, became assistant superintendent of the treasury (*gokanjōkata kogashirakaku*). By 1861, Ōkubo had risen to the high rank of *okonando* and became a major figure in Satsuma politics. This rapid advancement was unusual, especially for a lower samurai.[28] In March of 1862, Ōkubo, working through his high-ranking ally Komatsu Tatewaki, persuaded Hisamitsu to pardon Saigō Takamori, who had been exiled to a small island. Ōkubo and Saigō became the top Satsuma liaisons with the imperial court in Kyoto and negotiated the military alliance with Chōshū that provided the armed force to support the Meiji Restoration. Although Hisamitsu's earlier succession struggle with Nariakira has led later historians to judge him rather harshly as an obstacle to progress, his support of Nariakira faction reformers in the 1860s suggests that this caricature has been largely unfair.

In Nagasaki, Godai purchased a steamship that was named the *Tenyūmaru* for Satsuma in December 1860. This purchase marked Satsuma's renewed effort to build up its navy and coastal defenses. The expertise that Satsuma samurai developed in these early years would pay a great dividend later as the Japanese navy grew from these early beginnings. In fact, Tōgō Heihachirō, later known as the father of the Japanese navy and famous for his 1905 defeat of the Russian fleet, grew up in the same Kagoshima district as Ōkubo, Saigō, and Matsukata and studied naval science with Godai.

In January 1862, Thomas Glover, in violation of the bakufu's restriction on Japanese travel abroad, smuggled Godai to Shanghai. In Shanghai, Godai arranged for Satsuma's purchase of a steamship and its delivery to Kagoshima. In April of the same year, Godai returned to Shanghai to survey local conditions as a sailor on the bakufu ship the *Senzaimaru*.[29] Godai got a first-hand view of international capitalism through his contacts with Western merchants in Nagasaki and Shanghai. Wealth and power would have certainly been intimately connected in his mind after his study of Western naval technology at the bakufu school and his purchase of steamships with his domain's limited resources.

If Godai and other Satsuma samurai harbored any lingering illusions of Japan's current political economy repelling a Western attack, these evaporated on August 11, 1863 when a squadron of British warships sailed into Kagoshima harbor to exact reparations for the death of Charles Richardson whom Satsuma samurai had slain in an alteration. The Richardson Incident brought the reformist *kaikoku* faction back into the center of Satsuma politics. It also highlighted the precise nature of the challenge that Western capitalism and imperialism posed for Japan.

On April 14, 1862, Satsuma regent Hisamitsu left from Kagoshima for Kyoto with a thousand troops. Ōkubo had been sent ahead to meet with the court noble Konoe Tadahiro and prepare for Hisamitsu's visit. Together they hoped to work out a "union of court and shogunate" (*kōbu gattai*) to improve the imperial court's political position at the shogun's expense. On September 14, after escorting the imperial envoy Ōhara Shigetomi to Edo to meet with the shogun, Shimazu Hisamitsu's procession left Edo on its return trip to Kyoto.[30] Largely successful in his mission, he set out with his entourage of over 300 samurai along the Tōkaidō, the main route between Edo and Kyoto. Matsukata Masayoshi, who was later Minister of Finance in the Meiji government, was one of Hisamitsu's personal guards.

On that same morning, an acquaintance invited Charles Richardson, an English merchant, for a ride along the Tōkaidō to visit the British official at Kawasaki.[31] This stretch of the Tōkaidō was the cause of a good deal of consternation for the bakufu. The daimyo used the road for their processions to and from Edo to perform their ceremonial obligations under the alternate attendance system. The foreigners, however, had negotiated the use of the road in the unequal treaties. The bakufu asked residents of the foreign settlement to use discretion when encountering daimyo processions, but these warnings fell on deaf ears.

When the Richardson party reached the village at Namamugi, they encountered Hisamitsu's samurai procession. Trying to get out of the way, the party on horseback cut across the road and forced Hisamitsu's procession to come to a halt. Aroused by such a flagrant act of disrespect toward their lord, several Satsuma samurai drew their swords and attacked. Richardson was killed and two others were seriously wounded.[32]

British officials demanded satisfaction. In his dispatch to St. John Neale, Lord Russell called for an indemnity of £100,000 from the bakufu for not keeping its vassals in line. It also required Satsuma to pay a separate indemnity of £25,000 and execute Richardson's murderers in the presence of British naval officers. If these demands were not met, the chief officer of the British Navy in the China Seas would be authorized to take measures of "reprisal or blockade, or both."[33] Neale informed the bakufu, "Great Britain will not tolerate even a passive defiance of its power." This was the first British invocation of explicitly gunboat diplomacy and Neale had seven ships with over one hundred guns assembling in Yokohama to back it up.[34]

After the incident, Hisamitsu denied any knowledge of the men involved and hurried on his way in defiance of bakufu orders to turn over the assailants.[35] Richardson's assassins were asked to commit *seppuku*, but Ōkubo Toshimichi commended their loyalty and would not allow it.[36] In his report to one of Satsuma's branch families, Ōkubo wrote,

> The manners regarding daimyo are strict; even if it is a native who shows a lack of courtesy, it is the custom to cut him down. This is even more the case if it is a foreigner. Foreigners had been ordered not to go out this day because a Satsuma domain procession would pass. Because they did not listen to this and went out, the fault lies with the English. Is it not terribly rude to recklessly gallop on a horse toward a daimyo processional?[37]

Ōkubo clearly considered the British behavior toward the processional an outrage. His growing sense of nationalism was revealed in the phrase, "This is even more the case for foreigners." To him, foreigners had to adjust to the particular customs while in Japan. The Japanese need not adjust to some universal standard as dictated by the Western powers.

On August 6, 1863, Neale left Yokohama with the British squadron. Upon reaching Kagoshima on August 11, he presented Satsuma with an ultimatum repeating his previous demands. When he did not receive a satisfactory reply, the British tried to seize three steamships anchored in Kagoshima harbor to hold as payment against the indemnity.[38] Godai Tomoatsu was captain of one of these ships and was taken prisoner.[39] Ōkubo Toshimichi, by then a close adviser to Hisamitsu, witnessed the British seizure of Satsuma ships from the roof of the daimyo's mansion and gave the order for Satsuma shore batteries to open fire. Satsuma was using older round cannonballs, but good training enabled them to hit the bridge of the British flagship. The British, however, demonstrated the power of their latest Armstrong rifled guns firing cone-shaped shells.[40] In the engagement that followed, much of Kagoshima was destroyed and the British were forced to return to Yokohama to repair their ships. After the skirmish at Kagoshima, both sides claimed success and reached an agreement on December 11, 1863. Satsuma borrowed from the bakufu to pay the indemnity and promised to punish the attackers in the presence of British officers if and when they were found.[41] Godai Tomoatsu and the other Satsuma men who had been captured were released and quickly became leaders in Satsuma's efforts to further modernize its military defense.

The Richardson Incident and the Satsuma–British conflict underscored the need for more serious reform. Sakuma Shōzan had hoped for an accommodation between Japanese traditional ethics and Western technology. The Satsuma daimyo Shimazu Nariakira had experimented with Western technology while keeping the political order constant. Yokoi Shōnan had called for reforms that would promote wealth and power. In the wake of the Richardson Incident, it became clear to some in Satsuma that a more fundamental change in Japan's political, economic, and social structure may be necessary to function in an emerging world capitalist order.[42]

After the battle with Britain, Godai Tomoatsu and other Satsuma samurai recognized that Japan was militarily and economically unprepared to face the realities of international power politics. The expulsion strategy was proven useless, leaving opening the country as the only option. As a first step to shore up Japan's defenses, Satsuma dispatched a group of ten samurai to Edo to study gunnery in Egawa's academy, the same school that Sakuma Shōzan had attended a decade earlier. It was at this point that one of these students, Kuroda Kiyotaka (1840–1900), later the head of the Meiji state's development efforts in Hokkaido, began his rise in Satsuma politics.[43]

To pay for defense efforts, Godai submitted a plan to Satsuma officials in May 1864 calling for the export of rice, tea, raw silk, lumber, and maritime goods. He believed these ventures would generate the funds to purchase Western sugar refining technology and equipment. This would make Satsuma's existing sugar industry even more lucrative. The profits could then be used to buy necessary equipment, dispatch students abroad, invite technicians, and import military and mining technology to strengthen Satsuma.[44]

In the final section of this plan Godai wrote,

> Our domain's trade with Shanghai, Tianjin, and others would greatly increase and our technology would advance producing many benefits for the domain (*kokueki*). In this document, I have proposed that the domain's profits (*kokueki*) from sugar would quickly enrich the state (*fukoku*). As for strengthening the military (*kyōhei*), someone should be appointed to carry out this urgent task. Fifty or sixty talented students should be selected from the domain school (*Zōshikan*) and elsewhere and sent to the various Western countries. There they would study naval science, of course, as well as astronomy, geography, medicine, analysis, and other subjects. They would then return to teach others in various technical schools.[45]

Godai had a similar vision of economic development as Satō Nobuhiro, Zusho Hirosato, Shimazu Nariakira, and Yokoi Shōnan. Trade was the source of wealth. The domain could promote wealth through the acquisition of technical skills. To acquire these skills, bright students should be sent to places where the best samples of a given product were made. Once they mastered the necessary skills, they should return home and teach them to others.

It is also important to note that he follows Yokoi Shōnan in assigning to *kokueki* and *fukoku* nearly the same meaning. Technological advancement was also an important component of both commercial and military success. He mentioned naval science as just one of several technical skills that he believed the domain should acquire by dispatching students abroad. Writing to samurai officials, he naturally emphasized not only the military applications of foreign study, but also the importance of developing commercial opportunities were a consistent undercurrent. In fact, Godai would expand the *fukoku kyōhei* argument to the point of arguing that state power could benefit from fostering capitalist institutions and organizations.

Higher-ranking Satsuma officials found Godai's argument persuasive. On March 22, 1865, the domain dispatched nineteen samurai to Europe to bring back technical knowledge and skills to Satsuma. Since it was still against the bakufu regulations to leave Japan, Godai contacted Thomas Glover in Nagasaki to arrange their clandestine passage to Hong Kong. There they boarded a Peninsular and Oriental Steam Navigation Company ship bound for England. After passing through Singapore and the Mediterranean Sea, they arrived in South Hampton on May 28, 1865.

Apparently satisfied with the military knowledge he had gained in Nagasaki, Godai focused most of his attention, while in Europe, on technology to improve Satsuma's economic capability. Godai had specific instructions to observe British textiles, buy machinery, and hire foreign technicians. He bought nine spinning machines built by Platt Brothers and Company for £10,000 and hired seven British technicians to set them up. In June 1867, the Kagoshima Spinning Mill opened with 3,600 spindles run by steam. The Shimazu family operated the mill until it was sold in the wake of the Satsuma Rebellion.[46]

Godai's diary revealed his interests. His entries were most numerous regarding steam engine factories, sugar refineries, steamships, and textile mills. He hoped that these industries would promote Satsuma's economic advantage.

For example, he examined sugar-refining technology while in Belgium and wrote,

> On Friday, early in the morning, we went to look at steam sugar refining equipment. Inside the factory hall was a machine that would be of great use if brought to our southern island . . . Even on a smaller scale, it would greatly exceed our current production techniques and would prove of great use to our country.[47]

Godai was concerned with enhancing the productivity of Satsuma's sugar industry to provide more profits for the domain. He believed that the adoption of advanced technology was important, but Godai looked beyond technology as a quick fix. He realized that more fundamental institutional reform was necessary if the Japanese were going to compete with Western economic power.

Godai also took an interest in the history and overall conditions in the countries he visited to get a sense of what produced economic success. Of Belgium, he remarked,

> When compared to England, France, and other countries, Belgium might be called the smallest nation, but on the basis of national wealth, its prosperity greatly exceeds what one would expect of a small country.[48]

Godai must have had Japan in mind when he wrote these lines. Nothing could be done about Japan's size or natural resources, but if people from small countries such as Belgium and Britain could build up such wealth through shrewd trading, Japan could do likewise.

In France, Godai became acquainted with Count Charles de Montblanc (1833–1894). Montblanc had visited Japan in 1858 on the same ship as Baron Gros, Plenipotentiary of France. Upon his return to France, he tried to establish himself as a Japan expert acting as a go-between with the 1862 and 1864 bakufu visits to Paris. The Godai party stayed with Montblanc in Ingelmunster for two days. Next they visited Brussels to see the theater, call on a company producing steam engines, and explore museums.[49] Montblanc was an important source of information for Godai as he tried to make sense of European economic organizations and institutions.[50]

When Godai returned to Satsuma in 1866, he advocated opening Satsuma to foreign trade with even greater zeal. While in Paris, Godai agreed to establish a trading company with Montblanc. In their contract, Montblanc became Satsuma's agent to sell goods in Europe. Satsuma would send its minerals, cotton, textiles, wax, and tobacco and Montblanc would handle the exchange transactions.[51] Although the Meiji Restoration occurred before this plan could be put into operation, it signaled willingness in Satsuma to open to the outside world independent of bakufu policy.

In 1867, a Satsuma embassy attended the Paris World's Fair representing the "Kingdom of the Ryūkyūs." Montblanc facilitated Satsuma's participation in this event. Products from the Ryūkyūs were displayed under a specially designed flag. Next to them Satsuma products were displayed under the Rising Sun flag. Montblanc actively promoted the notion that Satsuma was a sovereign state in a confederation under the bakufu leadership.[52] The fact that Satsuma sent its own trade mission to the Paris exposition demonstrated that it considered itself a state in competition with others within Japan and with the West. Satsuma officials such as Godai Tomoatsu, thanks to the legacy of economic realism, were keenly aware that the power to preserve one's independence was intimately linked to a state's ability to promote trade and industry.

Godai and Montblanc also influenced a young Satsuma samurai named Maeda Masana (1850–1921), who would later be a key official in the Meiji government's Ministry of Agriculture and Commerce. Maeda became the apprentice of a Kagoshima scholar of Dutch Learning at the age of eight. Maeda's biographer Soda Osamu remarks that Maeda read what most *shishi* were reading including the works of Hirata Atsutane (1776–1843), Satō Nobuhiro (1769–1850), Hayashi Shihei (1783–1793), Sakuma Shōzan (1811–1864), and Hashimoto Sanai (1834–1859).[53] In 1865, he applied for permission to accompany Godai to Europe. Considered too young for the journey, the domain sent him to Nagasaki instead. In Nagasaki, Maeda studied English with the Dutch American missionary Guido Verbeck. Maeda also worked on a Japanese–English dictionary that was published in 1869 and widely circulated in Japan.[54]

Like Ōkubo and Godai, Maeda was convinced of the importance of developing wealth through trade. Shortly after the Meiji Restoration, Montblanc visited Satsuma to receive a decoration for his service to the domain. Maeda Masana joined him on Montblanc's return trip to Europe and spent seven years in France studying how to promote rural industries for export.

Conclusion

Commodore Perry's gunboat diplomacy forced thinkers throughout Japan to address the issue of Japan's economic and technological backwardness. Drawing on earlier realist domain development strategies, proponents of *fukoku kyōhei* argued for the adoption of Western technology and economic practices to serve Japan's national interest.

In Satsuma, Nariakira's death tilted the center of gravity in Satsuma policy toward fiscal conservatism. The British bombardment of Kagoshima, however, awakened even the conservatives to the perils of ignoring Western power. Godai Tomoatsu's 1864 proposal, journey to Europe, and subsequent activism all served to take Nariakira's vision of economic development to the national level. Godai observed that technical skill made countries great and even small countries such as England and Belgium could become world powers and command considerable respect if their peoples were industrious. History proved that a nation was not stuck forever in a certain state decreed by nature and that international power politics rewarded strength rather than virtue. Self-reliance and the vigorous pursuit of wealth and power seemed to be the only alternatives and Godai believed that learning new technology was the key to economic development and national power. The best strategy, then, was for the government to organize the people in the task of locating the best technology, learning it, and teaching it to others. This model of development was elegant in its simplicity and profound in its optimism. It was also very much in keeping with earlier development strategies that encouraged learning any skill that could produce products that would bring more bullion into the country.

Although state-guided expansion of trade was becoming widely accepted as the path to military power, we have seen that even future leaders of the Meiji Restoration were not yet prepared in the early 1860s to accept free market capitalism as an organizing principle for society. It was only when attempts to use Western technology to defend the Tokugawa Confucian order failed that leaders began to advocate even more radical alternations of Japanese institutions.

CHAPTER 5

Satsuma Leaders and Early Meiji Capitalist Institutions

The upheaval of the 1850s and 1860s allowed lower samurai such as Ōkubo Toshimichi, Saigō Takamori, Godai Tomoatsu, Matsukata Masayoshi, Kuroda Kiyotaka, and Maeda Masana to rise quickly in Satsuma politics. Ōkubo and Saigō were close advisers to daimyo Nariakira and later Hisamitsu. Godai traveled to Europe to investigate the sources of Western power. Matsukata, Kuroda, and Maeda each studied Western military science in Nagasaki or Edo. Satsuma's support of the imperial loyalist movement against the Tokugawa catapulted these samurai into national prominence. When they became leaders in the new government after the Meiji Restoration of 1868, members of the Satsuma faction were responsible for many of the most important economic policy decisions in modern Japanese history. Although their policies continued some of the themes of Satsuma's earlier state-centered economic ideology, they shifted toward a broader acceptance of private enterprise as the engine of future economic development upon which their nationalist aspirations rested.

The Western bombardments of Kagoshima in August 1863 and the Chōshū domain's Shimonoseki in 1864 forced a change in attitude among many samurai leaders. The radical xenophobic notion of "revering the emperor and expelling the barbarians" was no longer tenable and was quickly replaced with the more realistic "enriching the country and strengthening the military." Equally important was the shifting relationship between the domains of Satsuma and Chōshū that put aside their rivalry with each other and joined forces against the Tokugawa.[1]

In the summer of 1865, Sakamoto Ryōma, a samurai from the Tosa domain, arranged a meeting between Saigō Takamori of Satsuma and Kido Kōin of Chōshū, but this meeting ended without an agreement.

In January of 1866, Satsuma leaders decided the time had come for an alliance with Chōshū and sent Kuroda Kiyotaka to see Kido to make the arrangements. Later in October, Godai Tomoatsu met with Kido to establish a trading company between Satsuma and Chōshū.

By 1867, Ōkubo Toshimichi of Satsuma had established close ties with Iwakura Tomomi (1825–1883), a noble of the imperial court. Iwakura and Ōkubo shared a common vision of establishing a centralized state around the emperor and reducing the shogun's status to that of a daimyo. In the autumn, Matsukata Masayoshi acted as a messenger between Hisamitsu in Kagoshima and Ōkubo and Saigō, who were in Kyoto negotiating with Iwakura. On November 3, Ōkubo drafted a request for imperial orders for Satsuma to overthrow the shogun. The Tokugawa, he argued, had behaved selfishly by trying to preserve their interests while leaving Japan open to foreign attack. Their high-handed attitude had alienated the daimyo and, continued Tokugawa leadership, created the strong possibility of civil war that Japan could not afford in light of the foreign threat. Iwakura supported Ōkubo's petition and on November 9, an imperial order was issued removing Tokugawa Yoshinobu (*Keiki*) from office.[2] On December 18, 1867, 3,000 Satsuma troops under Saigō Takamori's command entered Kyoto and a *coup d'etat* was underway.

The Meiji Restoration was declared on January 3, 1868. At Toba and Fushimi on January 27, a combined Satsuma and Chōshū force of 6,000 defeated 10,000 bakufu troops. In April, Katsu Kaishū, the bakufu officer who had earlier studied naval science with Godai Tomoatsu in Nagasaki, met with Saigō Takamori to discuss the terms of the shogun's abdication. Fearing that a full-scale civil war would draw disastrous foreign intervention, Tokugawa Yoshinobu resigned as the head of the Tokugawa house and surrendered the Edo castle on May 3, 1868. Some of the Tokugawa allies refused to acknowledge the change of government and continued fighting in the northeast. In May of 1869, Restoration forces defeated the last resistance and ended the civil war.[3] On June 24, 1869, Ōkubo became one of six *sanyo* or junior councilors. The others included Saigō Takamori also from Satsuma, Kido Kōin from Chōshū, Gotō Shōjirō and Itagaki Taisuke from Tosa, and Soejima Tanemomi from Saga. Together they advised the court nobles who made up the emperor's senior councilors. Later in August, Ōkubo was promoted to the post of a *sangi* or state councilor.

After 1869, reform proceeded swiftly with remarkably little resistance. The domains were abolished and imperial prefectures were established in their place. Most daimyo were quite willing to give up their debt-ridden holdings in return for a guaranteed living and imperial titles. With the cost of prosecuting the civil war against the shogun's defenders and assuming the shogun's debts, the Meiji government found itself in serious financial trouble from the beginning. In the 1870s, the new regime focused on ensuring its own survival by securing a stable source of revenue with a nationwide land tax reform, eliminating the expense of samurai hereditary stipends, and promoting economic development to enhance the state's prestige both at home and abroad. Like earlier realist approaches to economic policy, the Meiji leaders tried to establish institutions that were appropriate to Japan's historical circumstances. To justify their policies, they repeatedly emphasized their contributions to national wealth and power. Some like Saigō Takamori continued to assert that state power should be used to uphold moral ends, but others like Ōkubo Toshimichi adopted the position that the state's survival and prosperity should be the ultimate end.

To solve its financial problems, the Meiji government began to cast a wide net for institutional models. One article of the Meiji Charter Oath, issued in April 1868, declared, "Knowledge shall be sought throughout the world so as to strengthen the foundations of imperial rule."[4] In this concise statement, the government demonstrated the strategic realist approach to institutional reform that had evolved from the late Tokugawa discourse on political economy. Government officials determined what action was appropriate to Japan's particular historical conditions, and once they had made their decisions, they repeatedly emphasized the contribution that their policy proposals would make to the state's wealth and power.

Approaching Capitalism from a Confucian Perspective

To make capitalism palatable to their contemporaries, many of whom continued to hope that Western technology could be used to defend Confucian moral principles, Meiji government leaders began to deploy economic nationalist arguments that put a new twist on the *keisei saimin* and *kokueki* terms that realist reformers in the late Tokugawa era domains had used to justify their policies. Liberalizing reforms were advocated not on the basis of individual gain, but rather on their contributions to national power and prestige relative to other countries. Confucian virtues of self-cultivation through education, sacrifice for the common good, and service to the sovereign were redirected to service of the nation-state (*kokka*, literally, national household) and influenced how the Meiji leaders understood Western economic institutions and articulated a consensus around capitalist economic development.

The Iwakura Mission was one of the Meiji government's most ambitious attempts to assess the actual conditions Japan faced and articulate an appropriate policy response. Between 1871 and 1873, the Meiji government sent many of its top leaders on a mission to Europe and the United States. Led by Iwakura Tomomi, Ōkubo Toshimichi, Kido Kōin, and Itō Hirobumi, the mission met with several foreign leaders to discuss the possibility of treaty revision. Although they failed to make any headway on the subject of treaty revision, Japanese government leaders did get a first-hand look at Western advanced technology, an experience that would have profound effects. Ōkubo became one of most enthusiastic supporters of importing new technology to Japan. On the Iwakura Mission, Ōkubo and others were able to compare the countries of the West to see that not all of them were advanced industrial nations. Many were still predominantly involved in agriculture. Others such as Prussia were in the process of moving from agriculture to industry. Japanese officials realized that industrialization was a process and if it was a process, it could be learned. As Ōkubo said in a letter home from San Francisco, "For our countrymen to learn the spirit of an open country (*kaikoku*) I hope that we will diligently research the various foreign arts of science, learning, production, manufacturing, and engineering so as to enhance enlightenment and excel in skill."[5]

Seeking to understand how an island nation might become a great power, the Iwakura Mission spent most of its time in Britain. The Japanese officials who were a part of the mission took detailed notes on every aspect of English life. Ōkubo was most interested in industrial production so he toured factories and shipyards to learn as much as he could about how England reached its status as a premier industrial power. In a letter to his Satsuma compatriot Saigō Takamori, now head of the government during the mission's absence, dated October 15, 1872, Ōkubo outlined his travels in England. He toured the shipyards at Liverpool, textile mills in Manchester, Glasgow steel works, and a sugar refinery in Greenwich. He also visited an Edinburgh paper mill, a New Castle steel works noted for production of Armstrong light artillery pieces, a Bradford cotton and woolen textile mill, a Sheffield steel works that manufactured parts for steam engines, and a Birmingham brewery.[6] From this list, we see where Ōkubo's principal interests were. He carried on Nariakira's concern with importing technology to enhance military preparedness. He also wanted the Japanese to improve their balance of trade by substituting domestic manufactures for foreign goods. To reach both goals, Ōkubo observed the best manufacturing technology available for industries that would suit Japan's circumstances.

It is perhaps no coincidence that leaders, wishing to put their observations of the West into terms easily accessible to Japan's samurai elite, chose a distinguished scholar of Confucian learning from Saga to be the Iwakura Mission's official secretary. In his account, Kume Kunitake (1839–1931), in true Confucian fashion, tried to understand the deeper principles behind what he observed. In Britain, Kume observed that wealth and technological advances were the products of customs and institutions that were fundamentally different from those in China and Japan. Kume wrote,

> In China and Japan, political principles have hitherto been derived from the customs of people who sustain themselves through agriculture and governments believe their main duty is to promote virtue have not taken the creation of wealth seriously. Lacking attention to these matters when establishing laws, there are no civil rights and no property rights. There is not only inattention to these rights, but also outright suppression as rules follow the whims of those in power . . . In today's world where trade relations are conducted through shipping, if a country is to have its full national rights (*kokken*) and preserve its national interests (*kokueki*), people high and low need to be united in paying careful attention to first enhancing fortunes and *achieving wealth and strength (fukyō wo itasu)*.[7]

In this passage, Kume noted the fundamental conflict of Confucian suppression of commerce in the name of virtue and establishment of property rights, which were necessary for modern capitalism. He also suggests that, although traditional Chinese and Japanese institutions may have been suitable in agricultural societies, the foundations of national wealth and power had clearly shifted to trade and commerce. Government policy would have to adapt to changing conditions and establish civil rights (*minken*) and property rights (*bukken*). Finding a way to put the principles of capitalism into language that an elite raised in the Confucian tradition could accept would be a significant challenge in the early years of Meiji.

Ōkubo Toshimichi and others in the Meiji government accepted market reforms and capitalist institutions of private enterprise as an ally in the ultimate goal of enhancing state power, but added that state officials should have the final word in determining what form Japan's particular capitalism should take. Ōkubo noted that Japan could not blindly follow models from any Western country. Japan would profit from learning a variety of technical skills, but, ultimately, the nation would have to find its own course. Later, in defense of state industries that liberals criticized on laissez-faire grounds, he remarked, "These industries are absolutely necessary even though they go against the laws of political economy." He added that Japan was "something different (*ibutsu*)" and needed "different laws (*hensoku*)" to make it develop.[8] This view of Japan as unique, having its own historical identity, became a consistent theme in Japanese political and economic nationalism. Tokugawa era Ancient Learning had emphasized the point derived from the Chinese Legalist tradition that powerful states were the products of sage leadership that established institutions appropriate for a country's land and people.

If Ōkubo found a vision of Japan's future wealth and power in England, he found the secret of how to realize this vision in Germany. Late in the Iwakura Mission, the Japanese leaders met with Chancellor Otto von Bismarck. In Bismarck, Ōkubo found a kindred spirit. Bismarck had recently masterminded the unification of Germany, which was now also engaged in catch-up industrialization. The parallels with the Japanese experience were obvious to the Japanese visitors. At dinner with the leaders of the Iwakura Mission on March 15, 1874, Bismarck gave his guests a lecture on the importance of self-reliance. Ōkubo recorded his impressions of the meeting in a letter to Saigō. He quoted Bismarck as saying, "Now the various nations of the world are all friendly and polite when they interact, but it is all only superficial. Underneath, reality is a struggle with the strong eclipsing the weak and the large scorning the small."[9] Clearly, Bismarck's Social Darwinist view of international relations as a battle for survival had a profound effect on Ōkubo and others on the Iwakura Mission.

Bismarck continued by telling them that a nation protected its sovereignty with power. If a nation only cultivated love of country without cultivating power, true independence would remain only a hope. Germany had secured her independence through military power and the productive capacity to support it. He concluded by saying, "Japan has many countries seeking friendly relations, but a country like Germany that values self-reliance should become the friendliest among the friendly nations."[10]

Bismarck's characterization of international relations and comments on the importance of power were, of course, not new to Ōkubo and the other leaders of the Iwakura Mission. The domains in Japan during the Tokugawa period competed with one other for wealth and power and recent Western behavior in East Asia confirmed the importance of strength in international relations. During their tour, the Japanese found that they had much in common with Germany. In the official report of the Iwakura Mission, Kume Kunitake wrote,

> The business of the Prussian people is heavily agricultural. Two million people, half of the total population, live in households where agriculture

is the primary occupation. As we should know from this country's trade with England, agricultural output is high and the surplus is sufficient to export. These profits are then used as a foundation for development of mining and manufacturing.[11]

The Meiji leaders understood that Japan too had to rely on agriculture to finance industrial development. The Prussians exported their surplus farm products to generate needed specie. This hard currency could then be used to import technology and equipment. The key to industrial development in these circumstances was the improvement of agricultural output. Kume continued by drawing a distinction between Prussia and other nations of Europe:

> Trade is carried out with foreign countries shipping goods even to distant lands overseas. This is different however from England and France. Both of these countries engage in maritime commerce importing raw materials from distant lands, adding their own country's manufacturing ability, and then sending them once again to foreign lands thus enriching the nation with profits from commercial markets. Apart from its military prowess, Prussia is not much written about in other lands. Yet, in building its national polity, it has a number of similarities with our Japan.[12]

The Iwakura Mission visit to Germany marked the beginning of an important transition in the Meiji Japanese search for appropriate institutional models. Since Godai Tomoatsu's earlier Satsuma mission to England, there had been a push to follow the British example and turn a small island nation lacking material resources into a mercantile power. Although they spent much more time in Britain than they did in Germany, many on the Iwakura Mission began to think of Germany's experience as a newly unified and late industrializing country as closer to Japan's own situation than Britain's. To scholars such as Kume educated in the Confucian tradition, the British and French were strictly mercantile countries pursuing nothing but profit. Prussia, on the other hand, seemed dedicated to using trade and industry to build its national polity and military strength. Capitalism was more palatable to Confucian sensibilities if it could be put in terms of service to national rather than individual interests.

In his report, Kume began by noting that Prussia's economic circumstances were similar to Japan's. Prussia was primarily an agricultural country and was industrializing to compete with England and France. These observations perhaps marked the beginning of a gradual shift in early Meiji economic thought away from the view that Japan was similar to Britain, the island-based empire. In its place, an understanding of Japan as a late developer like Germany that had to fight its way to power and prestige was beginning to take root. In the following passage, Kume explicitly contrasts the Confucian view of agriculture as the foundation of the nation's material and moral well being and the emphasis on manufacturing found in Western economics.

> In the Western countries, according to economists' arguments, a large agricultural population is not a beautiful thing to the nation. Rather, we should know the number of people engaged in manufacturing to form the basis for comparison . . . Each year, the number of Prussian people leaving their farming villages and taking up residence in the cities is increasing which is similar to England, France, and other countries.[13]

Here Kume observed that industrialization was a process. Traveling abroad, the Meiji leaders could clearly see that the nations of Europe and America each occupied a place on a continuum between agriculture and industry. Nations that were leaders in manufacturing such as Great Britain were powerful and commanded respect. Nations like Prussia that were still predominantly agricultural were moving toward industry as rapidly as possible. They further realized from their journey to the United States and Europe that most countries had just developed modern industry in the past forty years. The Iwakura Mission, therefore, further confirmed the notion, which had been evolving in the late Tokugawa period, that wealth and power were intimately linked; what made a country strong were the skill of its government's leadership and the diligence of its people.

In addition to travel abroad, the Meiji government also tried to understand Western institutions by collecting economics texts. The historian of economic thought Sugihara Shirō conducted a survey of the 1882 *Shokanchō Shozō Yōsho Mokuroku* (Catalogue of Western Books Kept in Government Offices) and found the following: Of the 2,170 economics volumes, 1,394 were in English, 567 were French, and 209 were German. English writers included liberal thinkers Mill and Jevons. American works included those by Francis Wayland, A. L. Perry, and seven books by the protectionist H. C. Carey. Lorenz Von Stein, K. H. Rau, W. G. F. Roscher, and A. H. G. Wagner of the German Historical School were all represented among the German works, but Friedrich List's main work was kept only in English translation until it was later translated by Ōshima Sadamasu. These books were held by seventeen government agencies, among which the Imperial University had the largest collection. The Ministry of Finance had the second largest library, which it used for reference and for educating future officials. After 1881, the number of German texts increased rapidly, as indicated in the "Author Catalogue of the Library of Teikoku-Daigaku" published in 1891.[14] Growing Japanese interest in German economic ideas in the 1880s seems to have coincided with Itō's study of German models as his officials drafted the Meiji Constitution issued in 1889.

Therefore, Japanese government officials had access to a variety of economic theoretical perspectives including the protectionist and economic nationalist views of Friedrich List (1789–1846), whose views were reflected in the writings of Ōkubo, Matsukata, and Maeda. List was an early proponent of protective tariffs to promote infant industries and national power. As professor of political economy at the University of Tübingen in 1819, List agitated for the creation of the Zollverein, a German customs union, and a protective tariff. The political authorities deemed his nationalist activities too radical and exiled him in 1822. He fled to the United States where he became an American citizen and was involved in the debate over an American protective tariff. His most famous work, *The National System of Political Economy*, published in 1841, became an important early text of the German Historical School of economics. List and the Historical School criticized Adam Smith, whose 1776 *Wealth of Nations* called on governments to minimize their interference in markets, and the British liberal economists for ignoring the fact that different policies were appropriate to different stages of economic development. Each nation had its unique history, the Historical School argued, so it was impossible to assert that free trade should be practiced universally.[15]

Japanese intellectuals outside the government also actively searched for new principles for Japan's economy. In their crusade to dismantle the structures of Tokugawa authoritarianism, liberal thinkers of the "Civilization and Enlightenment" movement such as Fukuzawa Yukichi and Taguchi Ukichi advocated free trade doctrines. Taguchi Ukichi (1859–1905) founded the liberal serial *Tokyo Keizai Zasshi* (Tokyo Economic Journal). Taguchi believed in universal principle and condemned the German historical view that economic policy might vary with the level of development. He also likened laissez-faire principle (*ri*) to earlier Confucian notions of enlightened rule.[16] This echoed the earlier Confucian debate over whether principle consisted of natural laws like gravity or whether it was a norm that manifested itself in different ways at different times. Kanda Kōhei (Takahira 1830–1898), who made an important contribution to the Meiji land tax reform of 1873, advocated free trade on principle, but recognized the need for government support for iron mining if necessary. He followed John Stuart Mill's utilitarian view that government entrepreneurial functions could be useful.[17] Fukuzawa Yukichi (1834–1901) moderated the pursuit of personal gain in his writings by focusing on Japan's independence and self-reliance. Fukuzawa apparently realized that Japan was losing in its foreign trade, but knew little could be done about it as long as Japan's tariff autonomy was restricted. In *Tsūzoku Kokkenron* (1878) Fukuzawa wrote,

> About foreign trade there is a theory that foreign commodities should freely be admitted so that anything that is inexpensive may be bought and consumed. Others, who are against this theory, claim that by importing manufactured commodities and exporting natural goods the nation cannot fail to lose profit that would otherwise be gained by manufacturing them and at the same time the manufacturing art itself . . . Therefore they are of the opinion that these imports should either be restricted or heavily taxed. I, for one, agree with this latter opinion, but because of the unequal treaties there is no prospect yet for any restriction to be adopted.[18]

With the Iwakura Mission's failure to revise Japan's treaties with the Western powers, the Meiji government was prevented from using tariffs, as advocated by Friedrich List, Henry Charles Carey, and other protectionist thinkers, to raise the prices that the infant industries could charge for their goods.[19] Since the Meiji government could not ensure profits for entrepreneurs in new industries by artificially raising prices, it focused instead on finding ways to lower costs for Japanese producers.

In *Minkan Keizairoku* (1880), however, Fukuzawa demonstrated a rather dim view of the government's ability to act as an entrepreneur. He conceded that the government should engage in those enterprises that "cannot be run privately without loss and at the same time cannot be left undone." But he continues,

> It would be a very great mistake to misunderstand this principle [of limited government economic activity] and believe that the government may do anything to enrich the country, running ordinary works and competing with people in trade and industry. Competition can only lead trade and industry to average prices and induce the parties concerned to every exertion. If there were someone who would do anything with no consideration of gain or loss . . . the effect would only be disastrous.[20]

Fukuzawa clearly understood the importance of the profit motive in economic activity. The government's ability to ignore economic incentives made it unsuitable to engage in business. But the key point here is "ordinary works and competing with the people." Fukuzawa was cautioning against the government's involvement in nonstrategic sectors of the economy. This differentiation between strategic and nonstrategic sectors of the economy was the central point of debate. Most intellectuals and government officials agreed that the government should only do what private entrepreneurs could not do for themselves.

Through the Iwakura Mission, study of Western economics texts, and the work of Japanese liberal economists, the Meiji leaders clearly understood the importance of private property rights and enterprise to economic growth. Yet, there was still a need to put these concepts into the terms of traditional values. Consequently, the 1870s were characterized by a paradoxical commitment to both clearing the way for free market capitalism as the engine of progress and government intervention to guide and nurture the people.

Establishing Institutions for Capitalist Economic Development

After the Iwakura Mission, many of the Meiji leaders accepted industrial capitalism as the best hope for a rich country and strong military to ensure the state's survival. The early Meiji reforms dismantled the Tokugawa feudal system and established some of the fundamental institutions of modern capitalism. In the early 1870s, the most pressing problems of the new state were how to solidify its monopoly on military force to quell potential unrest and how to generate sufficient funds to pay for it. The land tax reform of 1873 was not only crucial to establishing a stable source of revenue for the new government, but also confirmed property rights for land owners.

Matsukata Masayoshi, one of Ōkubo's protégés from Satsuma, entered the Ministry of Finance in summer 1871 and became head of the Ministry of Finance's Tax Bureau in 1874.[21] His views on the reforms were based in large part on Kanda Kōhei's proposal of 1870.[22] Kanda argued that the old Tokugawa era practice of collecting tax in kind according to a percentage of the harvest was too unstable for accurate government budgeting. Instead he recommended that the government collect taxes in cash according to a fixed assess value of the land. Consequently the taxpayer, rather than the government, would bear the risk associated with fluctuating agricultural yields and prices.[23]

In autumn 1871, Matsukata sent a memorandum to Ōkubo that outlined seven articles of his opinion on land tax reform. The document displayed a strong commitment to establishing a free market for land. In his first section, he wrote, "The cultivation of land should be entrusted to the free judgment of its owner." Matsukata argued that although domain lords had determined production in the feudal era, allowing people the freedom to cultivate what they wanted was consistent with "the government's own policy of foreign trade expansionism" and the "path of progress for the people's happiness and welfare."[24] Matsukata's statement represented the culmination of the gradual acceptance of the free market and it was now recognized as an ally in achieving state goals.

Second, "The sale and transfer of land should be permitted." When the previous regime attempted to regulate society by prohibiting the sale of land, Matsukata argued that people were evasive and there was no end to the state's financial difficulties. He concluded the section by saying, "The correctness of laws granting rights of ownership (*shoyūken*) and the freedom to buy and sell land should be well known." Matsukata recognized that property rights and allowing the land market to operate freely would actually enhance state finances.

Third, "Grain exports and imports should be allowed." Matsukata emphasized the importance of the profit motive in encouraging farmers to produce for export stating, "It is clear that farmers nowadays know the ways of agricultural business and are encouraged to produce what is profitable." To the extent possible, Matsukata believed that the government should rely on natural market incentives to achieve development goals.

Fourth, "Detailed surveys and land maps should be made." Here Matsukata asserted that the government had an important role in protecting freedoms and enforcing the property rights. "If the freedoms outlined in the previous three sections are simply left to the farmers and proper oversight is not established, we know there are cases when these freedoms can cause damage to the people's society." He went on to suggest that surveying farm land solely to raise tax revenue would meet resistance, but if officials could demonstrate that they were also protecting the farmers' interest, the state would enjoy the trust of the people and trouble could be avoided.

Fifth, in his section entitled "Determining the value of land," Matsukata condemned the old method of setting the value of the domain lords' (*kokushu*) lands based on tax quotas and called on the new government to devise a more equitable system of land valuation. In the sixth and seventh articles, Matsukata concluded that the land tax should be clearly determined as a function of land values and taxpayers should receive written deeds for their land, which would confirm their ownership rights. It might be a stretch to call Matsukata a laissez-faire capitalist, but his proposals showed a growing sense that allowing the market to operate more freely was in the government's interest.

Mutsu Munemitsu made a proposal in 1872 that was similar to Kanda's and Matsukata's, but differed on how land should be valued. Rather than using market prices for land, each parcel would have an assessed value based on its productivity. The Meiji leaders accepted this plan in June 1872 and Mutsu became head of the Tax Bureau in charge of its implementation.[25] This reform had the effect of confirming land ownership rights and material incentives for owners to increase agricultural productivity. Government officials assessed land values and issued deeds to the owners who would be responsible for paying the taxes. Establishing property rights for agricultural land was an important first step in Japan's capitalist economic development. As the economic historian Takahashi Kamekichi concluded,

> The result of the land tax reform was of course beneficial to the landlord's position and it has been argued that this played a role in capital formation that contributed to agricultural expansion. One part of the story of agricultural development in the first half of the Meiji era was the flourishing of land mergers and the appearance of large landlords, but fundamentally, it is about the landlord's capital formation—capital that would become the important wellspring of modern investment.[26]

Eliminating samurai stipends was another reform crucial both to improving government finances and to establishing productive economic incentives. The Meiji government inherited from the old regime's financial obligations for the hereditary stipends owed to samurai households. This proved to be a severe financial burden and the new Finance Ministry began to look for ways to quickly dispense with stipend payments. In 1871, members of the samurai class were allowed to engage in farming and commerce. Proposals were made to obtain foreign loans to pay off the stipends at a reduced rate, but were rejected. By 1874, optional commutation of stipends to bonds began and by 1876, commutation became compulsory.[27]

Ōkuma Shigenobu was perhaps most pointed in his call to end samurai stipends when he wrote in early 1876, "The time has come to reform the habits of the last several hundred years. Using valuable resources to nurture useless people should cease. Moreover, should we not say that this will result in the employment of unproductive people in productive enterprises for the benefit of the national state (*kokka*)."[28] For centuries, the samurai class had been considered the custodians of the virtues of self-sacrifice and loyalty. Now, in the government's view, they were use-less consumers of scarce resources. Merit, in Ōkuma's mind, had become defined in terms of material productivity in the service of the state.

In part to help the samurai make the transition to productive activity, Ōkubo Toshimichi in the early 1870s put his protégé Kuroda Kiyotaka in charge of the colonial development of Japan's northern frontier in Hokkaido and Sakhalin. In 1873, Kuroda suggested that the government could solve the problems of northern defense and samurai livelihoods simultaneously by recruiting warrior households to form military colonies in Hokkaido. Their principle occupation would be farming, but they could be readily called to military service in an emergency. Only 2,420 households were recruited in the decade that the Colonization Bureau existed, but it does show that government leaders were looking for ways to employ former samurai.[29] Kuroda hoped that the plan would also help diffuse growing tensions within the Satsuma faction between Saigō Takamori and Ōkubo Toshimichi. Saigō believed that the Meiji regime had mistreated the samurai class and hoped an invasion of Korea, in retaliation for the kingdom's refusal to sign an unequal treaty with Japan, would improve samurai morale. Ōkubo thought an invasion was too risky and called on the government to carefully consider the costs and benefits of the move. As Mark Ravina has shown, Saigō believed the moral principles of justice and honor took precedence over Ōkubo's fear of a budget deficit. To Saigō, Ōkubo had become "the biggest coward in Satsuma."[30]

To help entrepreneurs from the samurai and other classes establish productive enterprises, government leaders also moved to establish modern banking and currency systems. Itō Hirobumi studied the American banking system and wrote in 1870, "National banks (companies chartered according to paper currency regulations) as established in the United States are, when compared to various countries, truly the best system. If we can avoid some of the problems encountered in their original country as we establish them in ours, they can become in the future the foundation of a wealthy nation (*fukoku*)."[31] He early recognized that Japan benefited from other countries' mistakes and could improve upon institutional models as they were adapted to Japan's circumstances. He also believed that reliable institutions to provide currency and capital were important precursors to future economic development.

In the first decade of Meiji, the new government took major steps to dismantle the Tokugawa feudal system and establish new institutions that protected private property, ended many hereditary entitlements, and facilitated capital accumulation and market transactions. From these reforms, it is clear that the Meiji leaders had accepted market principles to a degree unprecedented in Japanese history. Yet Confucian moral sentiments did not disappear entirely.

Government Leadership

Despite their radical reforms, government bureaucrats in the Meiji era retained many of the moral convictions of earlier eras. They may have accepted capitalist industrial development as the means to national wealth and power, but many leaders continued to believe that the educated elite had a moral obligation to protect and guide the people. When the Iwakura Mission returned to Japan, Ōkubo Toshimichi was eager to put what he had learned abroad into action and became one of the most powerful supporters of rapid industrial development. He was appointed Minister of Home Affairs in November 1873 and cultivated the Japanese government's institutional capacity to guide the nation's economic development. Like Nariakira, Ōkubo's former lord in Satsuma, Ōkubo's vision of economic development included government leadership and Japanese adoption of the most advanced technology available. He called this policy *shokusan kōgyō* (promote production and encourage enterprise) and it guided the Japanese government through its early experiments with industrial policy. Yet, Ōkubo departed from earlier Satsuma practice in his acceptance of private enterprise as the engine of economic growth. Ōkubo and his protégés believed that government could provide an environment conducive to business and even take the lead in importing new technologies, but they recognized that the government's resources were too limited to develop Japanese industry on the old domain monopoly model.

Ōkubo worked with the other Meiji leaders to reorganize the government and articulate a vision of economic development. In November of 1873, the government brought local government, police, and industrial promotion together into one centralized bureaucracy. Ōkubo headed this new Ministry of Home Affairs and took an active interest in its industrial promotion bureau. His "Memorandum on the Promotion of Production and Encouragement of Industry" is a fascinating outline of the modern Japanese state's founding economic development principles.

First, Ōkubo recognized the importance of private initiative in economic activity:

A country's strength is dependent upon its people's prosperity. The people's prosperity is related to the abundance of production. And the abundance of production, of course, originates in the people's hard work in their enterprises.[32]

From Ōkubo's perspective, economic prosperity was intimately tied to national power. The Meiji government's goal was to enrich the lives of the Japanese people by helping them to produce as much as possible. The state was committed to the people's prosperity in enterprise, but within the context of serving the national interest as defined by government bureaucrats, not foreign economic theories.

Ōkubo made this point even more clearly in the next phrase of his memorandum, "However, if we explore the source of this hard work, it is none other than the energy with which government officials promote it."

Without government assistance, Ōkubo frankly argued, the people did not know what to do. This betrayed a rather dim view of the free market's ability to achieve the government's goal of rapid industrialization on its own. The government would have to intervene: "It is therefore the duty of state officials, wholeheartedly and skillfully on the basis of actual conditions, to encourage industry and increase production and thus secure the foundation of wealth and strength without delay."[33]

The government had a moral obligation to intervene in the economy to promote Japan's economic and military position in the world order. What is a little less plain is how they planned to do this. Ōkubo gives us a clue in the phrase, "on the basis of actual conditions." Meiji officials often used this wording to counter the liberal economists' theoretical arguments. The government would have to work closely with the Japanese private sector to solve real world problems. Ōkubo elaborated on this point as follows:

First of all, those responsible for the nation's subjects must take great care to determine the way, appropriate to the country's ways and customs and taking into account the people's temperament and knowledge, to conduct all affairs, from the [handling of] profits of industrial production to the operation of vessels used in land and maritime transport, that may be involved in the urgent task of protecting the people.[34]

According to Ōkubo, an economic plan, had to take into account Japan's particular historic and cultural circumstances. Japan was unique and could not be governed according to economic doctrines derived from other countries. It was up to the government's bureaucrats and not some universal set of economic doctrines to determine what would best serve Japan's interests. The Japanese people needed to be protected from the outside world and only the government could do that.

To illustrate his point, Ōkubo ironically drew an example from English history. In the 1870s, England was the premier maritime and industrial power in the world. After Adam Smith published his *Wealth of Nations* in 1776, many British economists and policy makers advocated low tariffs and free trade across national boundaries. The free trade treaty England forced upon China after the Opium War in the 1842 became the model for Western relations with East Asia. As a small island country that had grown into a world leader, Ōkubo believed, England provided an ideal model for Japan to emulate.

For guidance, however, Ōkubo looked not to contemporary England's laissez-faire policies, rather, he drew inspiration from England's mercantilist past:

> To give an example, consider a small country like England. The land of this island benefits from convenient harbors and is rich in minerals. England's government officials have built upon this natural advantage and have raised [their nation] to a magnificent level and fulfilled their enormous duty. Those government ministers, applying their minds together at this point in history, reaped the profits from world shipping. Wishing to greatly expand domestic industries, they resolutely established the special Navigation Acts long ago.

In this passage, Ōkubo argued that England had become the premier maritime power through the shrewdness of its government. The Navigation Acts prohibited the import of foreign goods unless they were aboard English ships. This policy served the dual purpose of promoting English shipping and protecting the domestic market from foreign competition. Intervening in a particular point in history, the English built upon their natural advantages and became the world's leading industrial power. From the beginning, the Japanese government's plan was similar.

Meiji officials such as Ōkubo Toshimichi had a keen sense of historical development. As times changed, different rules applied. They often spoke of reading the "trend of the times" (*jisei*) and adjusting their policies accordingly. Even at the beginning, men like Ōkubo did not expect Japan's protective policies to last forever. From the English example, Ōkubo realized that free trade served a nation's interests in certain circumstances:

> Since [the time of the Navigation Acts], England's industrial level has grown rapidly and has attained great prosperity with domestic production supplying the people's needs with excess [to trade]. Only at this point were restrictions abolished and free trade allowed. This is the source of England's wealth and power today.

Even in 1874, Ōkubo expected that free trade would one day be in Japan's interest. This had nothing to do with liberal doctrines of the mutual gains from trade. Rather, it was obvious that when a country's industry possessed competitive superiority, free trade policies would naturally follow.

Ōkubo was unimpressed with theoretical arguments and pointed out the hypocrisy of the Western powers calling for free trade in Japan:

> Most other foreign governments have protected their people and encouraged their industries in a similar fashion. Of course with difference in time, climate, and customs between East and West, we should not strictly follow England's actions. However, it would be a glorious achievement to build upon our natural advantages to expand wealth and strengthen the foundation of the nation.[35]

To Ōkubo, every country had to find its own path to modernity. Like the political economist Satō Nobuhiro had suggested to the Satsuma lord many years earlier, Ōkubo argued that the government should be active in coordinating the acquisition of technical skills. And like Satō, he made it very clear that economic growth was for the sole purpose of preserving the state.

Ōkubo's rhetorical style suggested that he was familiar with Friedrich List's protectionist arguments. List rejected Adam Smith's elevation of free trade doctrines to the level of universal principle. In his 1841 *National System of Political Economy*, List pointed out that the British had used protective measures during the era of the Navigation Acts. To List, it was sheer hypocrisy for the British to be preaching free trade to other countries now that they were the premier trading nation. Laissez-faire, it seemed to List, was simply an ideology that the economically strong nations used to keep the weaker nations in a position of subservience.[36] Germany, France, and the United States all chafed under British commercial hegemony in the late nineteenth century. Economic nationalists in each of these countries argued along the same lines as List and called upon governments to protect their domestic manufacturers against British imports. Ōkubo seems to have drawn on Western protectionist and economic nationalist ideas to validate and refine strategic economic policies that had evolved in Satsuma and other domains.

As Minister of Home Affairs, Ōkubo had the power to turn his economic nationalist ideas into policy when he launched his famous campaign to "promote production and encourage industry" (*shokusan kōgyō*). Government-run industrial works were the central feature of this program. Since silk was Japan's best-selling product overseas, the government began its industrialization efforts with improvements in the silk business. To mechanize silk production, the government established three modern reeling mills before 1880.[37]

The largest of these was the Tomioka Mill established in 1872 in Gumma prefecture. The government's public announcement clarified the plant's purpose. The poor quality of Japan's raw silk was unsuitable for use in Western textile mills and this resulted in the loss of valuable hard currency that silk sales generated for Japan. The government established the model silk mills not to make a profit, but rather to encourage private producers to adopt mechanical reeling. Anyone who wanted to open a silk mill could enter the plant and observe. Four hundred women would receive instruction in reeling techniques and then move to other districts to teach others. The announcement concluded, "By spinning high-quality silk, the government only wishes to give the people a profitable example."[38]

The government also tried to help Japanese cotton spinners overcome initial difficulties in producing high quality goods. Large initial investment was required to produce cotton thread on a sufficient scale to be profitable. Because coal was so expensive, producers relied on waterpower that was unpredictable and inconveniently located. Remote locations and high transport costs cut producers off from their markets. Workers had few traditional skills upon which to learn modern technology. All of these problems made Japanese production inefficient relative to their Western competitors.

Keeping with a strategy of import substitution, the government tried to assist domestic cotton spinning firms to compete with the imports that were flooding the Japanese market. In 1879, the government purchased spinning equipment from England with 20,000 spindles. The government established two other spinning mills at Ohira, Aichi (1881) and Kamiseno, Hiroshima (1882). The government also provided long-term loans to anyone importing spinning machinery. By the end of 1885, ten private mills had been established with machines the government bought in 1879 and three more with government loans.[39]

The government pursued a similar strategy in promoting the substitution of domestic products for Western imports. The popularity of Western dress and Western style military uniforms created a high demand for woolens. Between 1872 and 1877, woolens comprised 18.74 percent of all imports. To reduce the trade deficit, the Home Ministry established a large sheep ranch in Shimosa Province in 1875 and petitioned the Dajōkan to establish a woolen mill in 1876. This petition followed the same logic of many of the early Meiji industrial promotion projects. The Japanese, it argued, could improve their trade deficit by reducing the demand for imported goods. Reliance on foreign capital would sacrifice Japan's independence. Private Japanese capital was not yet strong enough to develop a woolen industry on its own. It was therefore necessary for the government to build and operate a modern mill. This would serve the dual purposes of meeting a portion of current demand for woolens and stimulating further private development of the woolen industry. The proposal was accepted and the government financed the construction of the Senju woolen mill in 1877 with the help of German technicians and machinery.[40]

Although it is clear, in retrospect, that private initiative proved much more efficient and successful than state enterprise in managing cotton and silk businesses, the model plants were still important. They signaled the government's commitment to new industrial enterprises that allowed private entrepreneurs to invest with greater confidence that their interests would be safeguarded. Ōkubo's *shokusan kōgyō* differed from Satsuma's industrial policy in one critical respect. Ōkubo believed that private enterprise should take over government projects as early as possible. The government would be the planner, facilitator and financier, but ultimately, Japanese corporations would have to do the work. Perhaps Ōkubo realized that private enterprise was a central feature of Western economic success and understood that the government's limited resources would be most productive if combined with private efforts. In delegating government projects to private firms, Ōkubo ensured that government goals were reached while private firms did the work in return for guaranteed profits.

While he hoped private enterprise would eventually flourish, Ōkubo, like many government officials of his era, had a condescending view of the Japanese people's ability to succeed in the international market. In his 1875 letter of inquiry of the supervision of commercial ships, he suggested that the Japanese people were still too docile to engage in shipping enterprises without government assistance. Yet, the government should be careful not to become overly involved and discourage what private initiative there was. A middle course of selecting a few able merchants for paternalistic government assistance, he concluded, was most suitable to Japan's stage of development. State assistance to successful private businesses such as Mitsubishi allowed these companies to gradually grow, by the early twentieth century, into powerful conglomerates known as *zaibatsu* (financial cliques).

Government support to these firms took the form of subsidies that lasted fifteen years and the transfer of government owned ships to Mitsubishi. Other shipping firms grouped around Mitsubishi to form a united front against foreign companies.[41] Mitsubishi's close relationship to the government was typical of the early Meiji government strategy to assist select companies until they could become strong enough to compete on their own. Iwasaki Yatarō, a samurai of the lowest rank in Tosa, founded Mitsubishi. The Tosa domain leadership recognized Iwasaki's talent and made him the head of the domain's industrial promotion office. When the domain was eliminated in 1871, Iwasaki converted the domain office into a steamship company. With government protection, Mitsubishi's steamship business quickly grew in the 1870s.[42] By the 1880s, the government encouraged more competition to lower freight rates and to keep Mitsubishi from exploiting its monopoly should a national emergency arise.[43]

Ōkubo did not stop just with shipping. He believed that Japanese trading companies were vital for gathering information about trading practices abroad. In 1875, he proposed that the government help establish a company for direct trade with the Western nations. Ōkubo based his recommendations on reports he received from Tomita Tetsunosuke who later became president of the Bank of Japan.

> Last October, Vice Consul Tomita Tetsunosuke returned from New York and reported on how our country's products are faring in America as stated below. He said that at the present time, the market conditions for the sale of our thread in America are gradually improving, but due to the frequently inferior and uneven quality of our goods, we can not erase the perilous doubt that has arisen in the Americans' minds.

Americans were prepared to buy Japanese products. The problem of poor quality threatened Japan's main export. Improving quality of exports, then, must be a chief concern among government officials.

The news from America was not entirely negative. Japanese tea was doing well as Ōkubo noted in the next line.

> Moreover, the Americans refer to tea produced in our country as "colorless tea." People in Boston generally love it and most people in Philadelphia are praising it. It will gradually spread to nearby areas and eventually spread to every state. This is certain. Recently, tea produced in China has included goods of terrible quality. The American people despise this and have grown to like our product. Therefore, if we send quality thread and tea and inspire confidence among the American people, it will not be

difficult for us to reap the profits in the American market which have hitherto flowed exclusively to China.[44]

Ōkubo argued that the government should act as a trading company and market Japanese products in America. In doing so, it could take market share away from the Chinese. Clearly Ōkubo had no sense of shared fate with the Chinese. He was perfectly willing to join the Americans in despising the Chinese and capturing the profits from trade for Japan. In his next section, Ōkubo made it clear that the government would take the lead in promoting Japanese products overseas.

> Considering this, there is no other time or occasion [than the present] to achieve the goal of opening the way for the flow of goods abroad and increasing the volume of exports. Tomita [Tetsunosuke] is of the same opinion. On this point, Tomita and I finally decided in November of last year that an industrial promotion official (*kangyō ryōkanin*) would be dispatched to America as his assistant. His main mission would be to report on that country's commercial conditions and to plan in detail ways to expedite the sale of our country's goods.[45]

After describing the difficulty that domestic producers have in getting their products to overseas markets, Ōkubo called for the creation of a government-sponsored trading company to reduce transaction costs for Japanese exporters.

> Now is the time for the government to take appropriate action and establish a foundation for direct sales abroad. The advantages of gradually expanding this base and extending commerce abroad and increasing the level of the nation's trade should be clear.[46]

While the government would sponsor the creation of a trade company, Ōkubo was quick to point out that private companies should operate it.

> This is not something that the government should do. Rather invite one or two companies, entrust to them appropriate capital, establish them at first in Yokohama and give them the duty of selling our products directly to trade companies from all countries. Later depending on how business develops, they can establish overseas offices and expand commercial operations both at home and abroad. These are the main points of my opinion.[47]

Even Ōkubo, who is typically associated with state activism, seems to have been trying to minimize the government's role. He clearly understood that competition between private firms was at the heart of Western economic development. Both British liberals and German economic nationalists acknowledged that individuals should own the means of production and private competition spurred people on to ever-greater achievements. The only question was how much the government should intervene to guide private competition toward meeting national goals. From Godai's studies in England in 1865 and Ōkubo' own journey in 1872, the Meiji leaders decided that the government should guide a private enterprise capitalist system rather than continue the Satsuma model of a state-run command economy.

With the government-assisted private company acting as an intermediary between Japanese producers and foreign merchants in Yokohama, the government could control the quality of products available for export. Eventually, Ōkubo hoped to circumvent the foreign merchants entirely and sell directly to buyers overseas. This would allow the Japanese to capture a larger share of the profit from export sales.

Ōkubo realized, however, that this plan would not be easy.

> But there are two difficulties. According to the actual record since the Restoration, few companies that have borrowed government money have done well and, based on that track record, we can not guarantee their success now. Also, if we take this action, it may end up hindering other merchants in Yokohama and resulting in conflict for profits between the people and the government. We also need to think about employment in the countryside. Whether the venture succeeds or not is related to how it is carried out and the personnel who do it. We should ask how we could give money to government enterprise and not private companies.[48]

Ōkubo was aware that government operations could choke out existing private initiative. He was also concerned with how regulation of silk quality would affect producers in the countryside. If the company refused to buy their silk, the livelihood of the rural producers would be in jeopardy. The key in Ōkubo's mind was recruiting talented bureaucrats to manage the government's relationship with the private sector and create incentives for Japanese firms to adjust their operations to the demands of export markets.

Conclusion

In the years following the Meiji Restoration, Ōkubo Toshimichi emerged as the leading proponent of state-led economic development. When he and his protégés encountered Western economic theory and practice, the new Meiji leaders interpreted it through their previous experience as domain officials and gravitated to those views that confirmed their prejudices. We would expect that economic nationalist rhetoric of state leadership, international competitiveness, and national power would appeal to former samurai officials struggling to solidify their new government's authority. What is surprising, however, is the extent to which they accepted the market as a force that could assist the Meiji regime in reaching its goals of national wealth and power.

What we see in the 1870s, therefore, is continuity of strategic goals across the Restoration. The government continued to assist construction of factories, shipyards, arsenals, railroads, and other facilities deemed necessary to jump start industrial development. But, there was an important change in the tactical approach to achieving these goals. Private property was established as the ordering principle of the economy as farmers were given land ownership rights, samurai entitlements were eliminated, and government enterprises were established based on their contribution to assisting private entrepreneurs in developing similar businesses.

CHAPTER 6

Establishing a Firm Foundation for Economic Development

Historians have generally considered 1881 to be a pivotal year in the development of the Meiji political economy. After a confrontation with the other oligarchs on the question of constitutional government, Ōkuma Shigenobu fell from power. That same year Matsukata Masayoshi became Finance Minister and began to privatize the industrial projects that Ōkuma and Ōkubo had built in the 1870s. This change in policy did mark a shift in government policy to a more laissez-faire approach to economic policy, but government leaders continued to argue that they had a moral obligation to protect and nurture the people as circumstances warranted.

One of the main reasons that the government was able to shift more of the burden of Japan's economic development to the private sectors in the 1880s was that counterrevolutionary threats had been effectively suppressed. The end of the Satsuma Rebellion not only marked the end of serious political threat, but it also showed how important expensive modern weapons and the revenue to pay for them was to the Meiji state. As the government's opponents shifted to agitation for democratic reforms and greater political participation, the oligarchs focused on improving economic conditions for the propertied classes that might consider joining the Popular Rights Movement.[1]

The suppression of the Satsuma Rebellion in 1877 effectively ended the discussion of samurai entitlements. Although the action put the government in a severe financial situation, its success allowed the government to quit its efforts to employ former samurai in state enterprises and focus on building the institutions of capitalism. Although this move away from direct government management of enterprises has sometimes been interpreted as a move to a laissez-faire policy paradigm, it is better understood as a shift in tactics rather than a change in strategic goals. Economic self-reliance remained a consistent objective, but the means to reach this goal shifted to establishing institutions that reduced costs for entrepreneurs and provided financial incentives for import substitution and export industries.

Although the Meiji government's victory in the Satsuma Rebellion removed the most serious threat the regime had faced, it was clear that political legitimacy was becoming increasingly tied to economic performance. People may have accepted the emperor as their sovereign, but the positions of those who claimed to speak in the emperor's name were contingent on the country's prosperity. The Popular Rights Movement was pressuring the government to produce a constitution that widened political participation beyond the oligarchy that had risen to power in the Meiji Restoration. Officials hoped that improvement in the people's economic prospects might lessen popular support for the government's critics.

By the 1880s, therefore, the Japanese government's economic ideology was committed to providing incentives for private capital to invest in industries that would have a positive effect on the country's balance of trade. Government leaders' understanding of successful government intervention was remarkably consistent on the themes of reducing imports and promoting exports. The open question was precisely how to do this. Despite expenses and setbacks of Ōkubo's *shokusan kōgyō* policies, bureaucrats from ministries most responsible for implementing these programs vehemently criticized any attempts to reduce government spending on these projects. Others, notably officials responsible for the government's treasury, believed that continued government investment in civilian industry was financially unsustainable. The tension between these two positions eventually yielded a synthesis. The government would continue to encourage import substitution and exports, but it would delegate as much of this effort as possible to private concerns. Without the burden of direct investment, the government could focus on reducing transaction costs with improved financial, transportation, and educational infrastructure.

In 1881, former Satsuma samurai Matsukata Masayoshi became Minister of Finance and added a new dimension to Ōkubo's industrial promotion program. Matsukata supported Ōkubo's strategy of import substitution and export promotion, but he recognized that financial solvency was also important in preserving Japan's independence. This meant that the government would have to cut expenditures and restore convertibility of Japan's paper currency to silver and gold.

Matsukata's policy of government fiscal austerity and reduction of the money supply induced four years of severe deflation from 1881 to 1885. The "Matsukata deflation" was not popular, but it was critically necessary for the Japanese to clear away the debts that were inherited from the Tokugawa and aggravated by the expenses of establishing a new government. As Henry Rosovsky has written, "Matsukata's policies jolted the economy, precipitating social disorder and political instability, but for five years he stayed on the same road, and by then the original government targets—adequate revenues, sound currency, modern banking—were safely and permanently achieved. The Matsukata deflation was strong medicine, but in our view, it had life-saving qualities."[2] Matsukata created the Bank of Japan to give the central government control of currency issue and to create the financial infrastructure for the development of Japanese industries independent of foreign capital.

Matsukata's colleagues from the former Satsuma domain made important contributions to the government's formulation of economic development techniques. Godai Tomoatsu, the leader of Satsuma's first mission to the West in 1865, wrote an "Opinion on the Rescue of Government Finances" (*Zaisei kyūji iken sho*) in 1880. Godai believed that the government should cooperate with private businesses to promote exports and domestic manufactures that could replace expensive imports from abroad. Maeda Masana, a junior member of the Satsuma faction, became a high-ranking official in the Minister of Agriculture and Commerce when it was formed in 1881. His 1884 "Opinion on the Encouragement of Enterprise" (*Kōgyō iken*) contained a comprehensive survey of Japan's existing industries and proposed that the government use financial incentives to promote the export of traditional products such as silk, tea, and rice.

In the early 1880s, the Meiji government was forced by financial necessity to sell state-owned enterprises to private entrepreneurs. Although this sale was a change of government industrial promotion techniques, it did not signal a dramatic shift in Japan's *fukoku kyōhei* economic development strategy. The themes of self-reliance and the encouragement of a positive trade balance remained an integral part of Japanese government policy.

Satsuma Rebellion

Clearly the samurai class had the most to lose in the early Meiji reforms and discontent was rampant in the early 1870s. Government leaders realized that pacifying this armed and potentially counterrevolutionary class was crucial to their political survival. When the Iwakura Mission returned to Japan in 1873, the Meiji government faced a crisis. The Japanese had tried to force Korea open to trade, but the Koreans remained adamant in their refusal. Saigō Takamori and Itagaki Taisuke, who had headed the government in Iwakura's and Ōkubo's absence, favored a Japanese invasion to force the Koreans to come to terms. Not only did they believe that military action would enhance Japan's international prestige, but they also hoped that an invasion would revive the samurai class that was largely unemployed after the Restoration.

Ōkubo Toshimichi opposed Saigō's planned invasion because it might invite Western intervention. Ōkubo believed that Japan had to concentrate on domestic reform to build up its industrial and military strength before becoming entangled in an international conflict. When their plan for an invasion of Korea was rejected in 1873, Saigō resigned from the government and returned home to Kagoshima.

The samurai as a class did not fare well under the Meiji reforms. When the domains were abolished in 1871 and imperial prefectures established in their place, the Meiji government inherited the domains' financial obligations. The largest of these obligations was the payment of stipends to the samurai. In 1873, the government began giving the samurai lump sums in lieu of their perpetual stipends. In 1876, all stipends were abolished and commuted to government bonds. The elimination of samurai stipends was crucial to the Meiji government's financial survival, but it was politically expensive.

Samurai discontent with the Meiji regime mounted and, in 1877, the Satsuma Rebellion erupted. In the Meiji Restoration, Saigō Takamori had agreed with his Satsuma comrade Ōkubo Toshimichi that the Tokugawa regime had to be destroyed. The two disagreed sharply, however, on what kind of order should take its place. Ōkubo's experience in Europe on the Iwakura Mission convinced him of the need for thorough reform that would include the elimination of samurai privilege. Saigō, on the other hand, advocated moderate reform and the preservation of the samurai class. Many disaffected samurai joined Saigō after he left government service over the Korean invasion controversy. When the Meiji government cut their stipends, 40,000 samurai joined Saigō in an uprising against the government he had fought to create.

The Meiji government's newly created conscript army of mostly peasants proved to be an effective force in the Satsuma Rebellion. The army soundly defeated the rebels and Saigō Takamori committed suicide on the battlefield near Kumamoto castle in September 1877. The peasant army's victory destroyed the samurai class and solidified the early Meiji reforms. To pay the expenses of putting down the Satsuma Rebellion, the Meiji government issued 27 million yen in bonds. Combined with the 172.9 million in bonds that the government had earlier issued for the commutation of samurai stipends, this contributed to a rapid inflation in the money supply. Between 1876 and 1878 the supply of government paper money and national bank notes in circulation rose to 55 percent.[3]

To make matters more uncertain for the government, some of Saigō's sympathizers attacked and killed Ōkubo Toshimichi's in his carriage when he was on his way to his office on the morning of May 14, 1878. With Saigō's death in battle, and Kido Kōin's fall to illness, the "triumvirate of the Restoration" was no more. A struggle for top leadership began almost immediately between Itō Hirobumi from Chōshū and Ōkuma Shigenobu from Hizen. Ōkubo's patronage had made Ōkuma the Minister of Finance for much of the 1870s and it fell upon him to solve the financial crisis in the wake of the Satsuma Rebellion.

Ōkuma shared Ōkubo's basic belief that the promotion of export industries to bring specie into Japan was the best way to improve the nation's economic condition. To Ōkuma, inflation was caused not so much by an oversupply of paper currency as an undersupply of specie to back that currency. The government should, therefore, *increase* the level of available credit to producers so that they could expand their production of export commodities. If they did that, specie would flow into Japan and the currency problem would take care of itself. Ōkuma's short-term solution was to borrow funds from abroad to back Japanese paper currency and then repay the loans with revenue that Japanese exports would generate Matsukata Masayoshi from Satsuma, who would later become on of Japan's most influential Finance Ministers, differed sharply with Ōkuma as to how to best reach the government's *fukoku kyōhei* goal.

Financing Growth

In 1880, the Japanese government stood at a crossroads with respect to economic development. Inflation was out of control after the government paid for the suppression of the Satsuma Rebellion with inconvertible paper currency. Finance Minister Ōkuma Shigenobu continued Ōkubo's policy of providing easy credit to industry. He hoped this would stimulate exports and bring in needed specie to back the paper currency that was already in circulation. To tide the government over in the meantime, Ōkuma proposed to borrow money in London. Matsukata Masayoshi vigorously opposed this move because it would sacrifice what little independence Japan had left. This issue together with a political confrontation with Itō Hirobumi over constitutional government forced Ōkuma out of the government in 1881. Replacing Sano Tsunetami, who served for several months as Minister of Finance after Ōkuma, as Finance Minister, Matsukata changed the direction of the government economic strategy from direct promotion of targeted industry to indirect encouragement through financial incentives. With the counterrevolutionary Satsuma Rebellion suppressed, the Meiji government was in a stronger political position to induce the private sector to bear a greater share of industrial development expenses.

Matsukata, like Ōkubo, was from Satsuma's Nariakira faction. He was sent under domain orders to study naval science in Nagasaki on the eve of the Meiji Restoration. After the Restoration, he served briefly as the governor of Hida (now part of Oita) prefecture in northern Kyushu before being summoned to the new central government's Finance Ministry. In the 1870s, Matsukata worked on financial issues in several posts in the new government. Like many of Japan's leaders he was concerned with the unfavorable trade balance in the 1870s. Since tariffs were under international control, the only way to reduce Japan's trade deficit was for Japanese industry to become competitive. As he wrote in 1875,

> If we henceforth make every effort to increase production and reduce imports, we may confidently expect such growth of industrial production that after a decade financial stability will be achieved as a matter of course. If we fail to do this, however, and continue to buy imported goods with specie, our government and people may give the appearance of making progress, but the reality will be quite different.[4]

This passage clearly showed Matsukata's economic nationalist views. Although newly industrializing countries often ran a balance of payments deficit while they are importing expensive capital equipment and building infrastructure, Matsukata understood indebtedness as a form of servitude. Matsukata cited the bakumatsu scholar of Dutch Studies Yamamoto Kakuma (1828–1892) as an important influence of his financial orthodox emphasis on balanced government budgets. Yamamoto from the Aizu domain was captured during the 1868 Meiji Restoration forces' conflict with the Tokugawa and was kept several months as prisoner in the Satsuma mansion in Kyoto. During his captivity, Yamamoto, unable to write due to an eye disease, dictated his views on state formation, international trade, banking, currency, and other policy issues.[5]

Matsukata's trip with the Japanese Delegation to the International Exposition in Paris in 1878–1879 gave him new insights into how to deal with Japan's developmental problems. There he sought out Leon Say who had been France's Finance Minister (1872–1879).[6] During this time, the French had recovered from their defeat by the Prussians in 1871, having paid a £200 million indemnity. Say's secret was a convertible currency backed by gold, which gave the state sound credit and respectability. Balanced budgets were also important because states with good credit could issue bonds to finance their needs.[7] The importance of sound finance and creditworthiness would become the dominant themes in Matsukata's career as Finance Minister.

For Matsukata Masayoshi, self-reliance and orthodox finance were not only a matter of good policy, but were also profoundly personal. When Matsukata was a young man in Satsuma, his father who had been the supervisor of the gunnery works at Kagoshima died, leaving the family a large debt. Considering repayment a point of honor, Matsukata's family worked hard. Matsukata considered the suffering that his family endured to pay off the debt his father left when he died to be an important event in his life. He would recall in later life that the day he paid off the debt was "one of the most satisfying moments of his whole career."[8]

During the 1877 Satsuma Rebellion, the government suspended convertibility of bank notes to specie and used inflation to finance military action. After Ōkubo's assassination in 1878, Finance Minister Ōkuma Shigenobu continued his basic financial policy. Ōkuma did not consider inflation to be a danger. He believed that the lack of silver in Japan rather than an overabundance of paper currency caused inflation. If more money could be channeled into Japan's export industries, specie would flow into Japan and the currency problem would be solved. To provide the initial capital for this plan, Ōkuma proposed to borrow money in London.

While still Home Minister, Matsukata submitted a proposal "Outline of Public Finance" (*Zaisei kanki gairyaku*) in June 1880. This critique of Ōkuma's proposal to solicit foreign loans to back Japan's currency outlined the basics of Matsukata's strategic thinking. The opening sentences gave plenty of warning of what was to come.

> Councilor Ōkuma Shigenobu's proposal for the reform of the currency system is, thinking in terms of theory, in keeping with the original specie system and is therefore well and fine to say. But, it is not at all appropriate to reality and is at odds with the trend of the times. Furthermore, to put it into action would be difficult, even dangerous. The accumulation of foreign debt is easy to begin but difficult to end. It is my heartfelt opinion that we must consider the future and decide against this proposal today.[9]

There were, of course, important political motivations behind Matsukata's attack on Ōkuma's policies. It sent a clear signal that Matsukata was backing Itō against Ōkuma in the power struggle that followed Kido's and Ōkubo's deaths. Nevertheless, the grounds upon which Matsukata based his attack were consistent with his earlier economic nationalist positions. First, policy should be judged pragmatically on its effect on the national interest. Correct policy according to Matsukata must be in line with the "trend of the times" (*jisei*). Under normal circumstances, borrowing abroad was an accepted practice in economic theory. Japan's historical circumstances, however, necessitated a different approach. Second, Matsukata took the nationalist position that borrowing abroad at high rates of interest severely weakened Japan's ability to be self-reliant even though liberal theory suggested that it was natural and beneficial for capital to flow freely from rich to poor countries.

In 1881, Matsukata elaborated his opposition to deficit finance and loans from abroad.

> The government's purpose above is undecided; the people's hearts below are wavering. High and low together are tossed left and right by the flow of the times and have no way to snatch a moment's rest to catch their breath. To ensure financial health and avoid danger in the future, we must not entertain the notion of seeking foreign capital. There is more than one person talking about this idea and if it is put into action, it will certainly meet disaster. Look at our country's actual experience! Whether it is our tariff rights or our legal rights, not one single thing has been returned. We are in a poor and helpless position. When we seek capital together with knowledge and economic power from the wealthy foreigners and disperse it in our country, in spite of the benefits of a momentary infusion of specie, it will cause us great injury and disease. This should be clear without saying so. As one might expect, the country's goals will not be achieved. If this policy is adopted at this time, it will come to naught. The entire country's condition will shift and sink to the condition of Egypt, Turkey, or India. Should we not consider [the consequences of the proposal to borrow abroad] and not stand idly by with hands folded while this happens?[10]

Matsukata again emphasized the theme of self-reliance. Japan, he argued, was in a perilous position forced to seek "knowledge and economic power from the wealthy foreigners." If Japan also borrowed capital, the nation would be submitting to foreign control. Matsukata clearly had a hierarchy of nations in mind. The world was divided between masters like Britain and France and slaves like Egypt, India, and Turkey.

Although these countries were once great civilizations, they had given away their rights and served the great powers. The great powers, on the other hand, never gave back anything that they had taken. Matsukata urged his colleagues to consider what Japan in her weakness was forced to give up. The unequal treaties of 1858, which put Japan's tariffs under international control and exempted foreigners from obeying Japanese law while in Japan, were still in effect two decades later. If the Japanese stooped to borrowing money from abroad, Matsukata believed, there would be no end to these insults to Japanese national sovereignty and dignity.

Once Matsukata reiterated the need for self-reliance, he followed another well-worn pattern of strategic economic policy. In his "Outline of Financial Policy," he took stock of Japan's actual historical circumstances and formulated a plan to maximize the inflow of specie into Japan's money supply.

> The current issue of paper currency is really as much as 110,000,000 yen. This would be extremely difficult to convert to specie. Therefore, we must first raise as preparation funds around 10,000,000 yen and print another 15,000,000 yen in public bonds. We must support a reduction of the present amount of paper currency. In conjunction with this, we must increase the level of specie reserves gained from foreign trade.[11]

Matsukata's strategy had two components. First he worked to reestablish currency convertibility to safeguard the property rights of creditors and create stronger incentives for more productive investment. Second, he believed that convertibility required improving Japan's balance of trade to bring in enough specie to back paper currency.

Matsukata then surveyed the government's current financial position and took stock of all available sources of specie including 250,000 yen from tariffs, 500,000 yen from government mines, and 500,000 yen from mines operated by Shimazu Tadayoshi and Godai Tomoatsu. The Kōgyō Company, financed directly by Yokohama Specie Bank, was shipping coal to China and generating 1,000,000 yen a year in specie. The government's Miike mine also sold coal to China, generating 500,000 yen per year. Matsukata argued that these transactions should be conducted in Shanghai and the specie sent straight to London to settle Japan's foreign exchange obligations.[12] Matsukata continued the economic nationalist preoccupation with trade and currency flows. Accumulating specie to finance Japan's needs was Matsukata's overriding concern. After figuring out the sources of specie, Matsukata inventoried the revenue from raw silk and tea exports and came up with a total of 2,500,000 yen. This too, he argued, should be sent overseas as foreign exchange to reduce Japan's trade deficit.[13]

Inoue Kaoru, one of the oligarchs from Chōshū, agreed with Matsukata and submitted his own memorandum on financial reform in August of 1880. Inoue outlined a plan to improve Japan's trade budget by reducing government spending. He proposed that the government substitute domestic manufactures for costly imports of equipment for the army, navy, and government industry. Inoue also called upon the government to establish a Bank of Japan to provide easy credit to exporters. The government, he argued, should also encourage the development of Japanese trading and insurance companies to avoid costly foreign services and reduce transaction costs for exporters.[14]

In 1880, Godai Tomoatsu also wrote an opinion on how to best solve the government's debt and inflationary problems. As a Satsuma samurai, Godai led students to Europe in 1865 served as an officer in Satsuma's newly created navy, and worked to establish a trading company in cooperation with Count Montblanc. After the Meiji Restoration, Godai became an official in the new government's Osaka metropolitan administration. In 1869, Godai left the government, but remained close to Ōkubo Toshimichi and other government leaders. With government connections, Godai became a successful entrepreneur and leader in the Osaka business community. He also helped to establish the Osaka Chamber of Commerce and the Osaka Stock Exchange in 1878.

Godai's "Opinion on the Rescue of Government Finances" (*Zaisei kyūji iken sho*) began with the basic mercantilist premise that a trade deficit was the root of all evil. Godai argued that the return of Japan's "trading rights" or tariff sovereignty was of paramount importance. The government could then use tariffs to protect Japan's emerging industries. In the meantime, the government would have to find other ways to encourage export and import substitution industries. Once the trade balance improved, Godai believed specie would flow into the country and the convertibility of paper currency could be restored.[15]

Godai divided his proposal into two sections, one on import substitution and one on export industries. In the import substitute section, Godai outlined ways for the government to assist cotton spinning, sugar, petroleum, mining, and other industries. To assist cotton spinners, Godai proposed two ideas. First, the government should make loans for working capital to those who had already bought machinery up to 80 percent of the machinery's value. Second, the government should acquire machinery and sell it at reduced price to those who wished to set up cotton spinning mills. For sugar producers, Godai made a similar proposal that the government provide financing for land to cultivate sugar cane and the machinery to refine it. Godai proposed that the government sell its mines to private entrepreneurs to encourage the growth of a domestic mining industry. In each of these cases, Godai justified the government's assistance of private entrepreneurs with the economic nationalist logic that domestic production of the country's needs was preferable to importing goods from abroad.[16]

In his section on export promotion, Godai made proposals to assist the silk, tea, and shipping industries. He also called on the government to expand roads, harbors, and other transportation infrastructure. The uneven quality of Japanese silk reduced its value because mechanized Western silk mills required uniform raw materials. Godai called for the government to acquire and sell machinery to entrepreneurs for spinning silk thread to improve its quality. Godai believed that government support was critical to the success of private businesses seeking to compete with Western products either at home or abroad.[17]

Comparing this 1880 proposal with Godai's earlier petition to the Satsuma government in 1864, reveals some consistent themes.[18] First, Godai's belief in the importance of government leadership in the economy permeated both documents. These are not the writings of a frustrated member of the bourgeoisie trying to break free from feudal restrictions. Rather Godai had a vision of close state–mercantile cooperation to achieve their shared goal of a prosperous country. Second, Godai followed the economic nationalist pattern of judging the importance of industries based on their contribution to improving the country's trade balance. In contrast to laissez-faire liberalism, the nation rather than the individual should maximize its profits.

In 1880, Ōkuma Shigenobu exposed Kuroda Kiyotaka's proposed sale of government assets in Hokkaido at extremely low prices to a group of entrepreneurs led by Satsuma crony Godai Tomoatsu. Ōkuma's attempt to rally support against the Satsuma and Chōshū factions by appealing to popular opinion, together with his liberal political views provoked Itō and other leaders to force him out of the government. When Matsukata became the Minister of Finance in 1881, he began to privatize the government operated model factories, just as Godai had earlier suggested.[19]

Matsukata's sale of the pilot factories, therefore, did not constitute a shift to laissez-faire ideology. Rather, it was very much in line with the economic nationalist strategy of accumulating specie at all costs. To prosper in trade, Matsukata believed that Japan required first a sound financial system.

As Matsukata himself said,

> If we want our country to be open and progressive and compete with the great powers, we must complete the work of establishing Western systems. Consequently, we must recognize that the expenses necessary to do this are increasing very rapidly. The Dajōkan currency now issued responds to this, but does not constitute a sound fundamental policy. A fundamental policy nurtures true power (*jitsuryoku*) and advances national wealth. If we want to nurture true power and advance national wealth, we must encourage an industrial promotion (*shokusan kōgyō*) policy.[20]

In this Matsukata recognized the need for the encouragement of industry, but it would have to be done without resorting to deficit finance through inflation.

When Matsukata Masayoshi became Finance Minister in 1881, he set targets of sound convertible currency, adequate revenues, and a modern banking system. In 1884 the price level was down to 75 percent what it had been in 1881 and by 1885, the supply of money had fallen 20 percent.[21] Matsukata, therefore, used conservative finance to restore faith in the Japanese currency. Although the direct government role in the management of nonmilitary enterprises was reduced, it still was an important source of capital for private firms. The banking system that emerged out of the Matsukata deflation policies provided the institutional mechanism to unite savers and investors. The sale of the government sponsored model factories at nominal prices provided private entrepreneurs a head start to profitability. All of this suggests that Matsukata believed that successful development depended mostly on private enterprise, but that the state had to be ready to render aid when necessary.

In his March 1, 1882 memorandum, Matsukata argued that the central bank should be allowed to discount bills and make short-term loans at lower than market interest.

> In this way the [private] bank would be able to tide over the period of stringency, and avoid causing panic or coming to bankruptcy. But the services of a central bank will not be confined to its lending assistance to other banks. Private corporations and companies engaged in business enterprises or in manufactures, may also receive its assistance and pass through times of distress, without being reduced to the last necessity of making retrenchment either in the volume of business or in the scope of enterprise.[22]

The Bank of Japan, in Matsukata's thinking, would play an important role in the finance of economic development. As a central bank, it would lend to other banks during times of financial contraction. It would also loan to businesses that the government wished to assist. Matsukata intended for the central bank to work together with two other government financial institutions, a savings bank and an industrial bank. In his 1882 memorandum to establish the Bank of Japan, he wrote the following:

> Industry and thrift are two chief factors in the production of national wealth, and the savings bank has for its aim the encouragement of the spirit of thrift, while the industrial bank seeks to encourage industry among the agricultural and manufacturing classes. And what the industrial bank seeks to do among the agricultural and manufacturing classes, the Central Bank tries to accomplish among the commercial classes . . . They may be compared to three feet of a tripod which support the economic structure of the nation.[23]

In this, we see the twin pillars of economic nationalist thinking. Saving and investment in productive enterprises had been government business in Satsuma. After the sale of the pilot plants, a larger share of this responsibility was delegated to the private sector. Using affiliated financial institutions, the government could promote its economic development objectives at a much lower cost than direct operation of enterprises.

Thus, we see that Matsukata changed the government's tactics without altering the fundamental development strategy. The government was not wedded to the notion of state enterprise. These existed from the beginning to provide technical instruction to the private sector. The main goal was the maximization of specie flowing into Japan. If this goal could be continued at reduced expense to the government, so much the better.

In spite of the general impression that the sale of the pilot plants and the Matsukata deflation represented a move toward laissez-faire capitalism, this is not the whole story. Several recent Japanese studies show that the Meiji government's 1880s and 1890s military build up financed with bond issues had the same effect as a direct industrial policy in stimulating modern import substitution and export industries.[24]

In spite of earlier protests against borrowing abroad to finance the Japanese government's needs, Matsukata changed his position in the early 1880s. In October 1883, Matsukata authorized the Yokohama Specie Bank to approach foreign merchants to borrow one billion dollars to gather specie to restore Japan's currency convertibility. In April 1884, the Bank of Japan issued bonds valued at 100 yen to be sold for 90 yen in London through Watson, a British merchant residing in Yokohama. That October, negotiations for a bond sale of 2 billion yen broke down, but in March 1885, Bank of Japan President Yoshihara Shigetoshi was dispatched to London to issue 1 to 2 billion yen in gold denominated bonds discounted from 100 to 90 yen at an exchange rate of 5 silver yen to the pound. This attempt also failed because of uncertainty in the price of silver relative to gold. Consequently, the government had to rely primarily on domestic bond issues to finance currency reform and railroad construction.[25] When we look behind the nationalist bluster that political discourse of the day required, we see that one of Matsukata's driving concerns was improving the Japanese government's ability to borrow abroad on advantageous terms.

Lingering Moral Responsibility to Nurture the People

As if to prove that the government was not abandoning the promotion of industry with the sale of the pilot plants, the Meiji leaders created the Ministry of Agriculture and Commerce in 1881. Maeda Masana (1850–1921), who became a senior official in the new ministry, continued Ōkubo's comprehensive vision that promoted both traditional and modern industry. His emphasis, however, was on strengthening the traditional base of the economy so the people's savings could be funneled into development projects.

Maeda grew up in Satsuma as the apprentice of a scholar of Dutch Studies and applied to join Godai Tomoatsu on the 1865 Satsuma Mission to Europe. Senior Satsuma officials considered Maeda too young at fifteen for the journey and sent him to study in Nagasaki. Shortly after the Meiji Restoration conflict ended in 1869, the new government sent Maeda to France through Godai's contact, Count Montblanc.

Montblanc traveled to Japan after representing Satsuma in the 1867 world fair.[26] In December 1869, Montblanc returned to Paris and established a consulate to carry out business for the new Meiji government. Having met Maeda Masana who had traveled to France aboard the same ship, Montblanc employed him as a secretary. Maeda lived in the Montblanc residence while he attended classes and worked in the consulate.[27]

On July 19, 1870, the Franco-Prussian War broke out. Experiencing the ensuing siege of Paris, Maeda realized that Western civilization was far from perfect. During the siege, food ran short and order began to break down. Napoleon III was arrested and a republic declared. In the pandemonium that war brought to France, Maeda realized that it was not weapons or military organization that mattered so much as the discipline and morale of the troops.[28] If the political and social foundations of the nation were weak, no amount of military technology could produce strength.

This proved to be a crucial realization for Maeda that was to define the rest of his career. The people's spirit was intimately connected to their material well being. If individual lives were chaotic and unproductive, the nation had no source of strength in times of economic or military pressure. The source of *"fukoku kyōhei"* for Maeda then was where most of the Japanese people lived, in the countryside.

When the Iwakura Mission visited France in 1872, Ōkubo Toshimichi met with Maeda and other students from Kagoshima who had formed the "Hometown Friendship Club." The encouragement of such a high official in the new government must have left a deep impression upon these young students.[29] As the leader of the Satsuma faction in the Meiji government, Ōkubo cultivated the talents of his young protégés.

With renewed government support, Maeda began to study with Eugene Tisserand (1830–1925). In 1871, Tisserand had entered France's Ministry of Agriculture and Commerce and was promoted to Vice Minister in 1874.[30] Tisserand advocated a holistic approach to development. England had concentrated on manufacturing and had a much smaller agricultural population than France and Germany. To catch up, countries with large agricultural populations had to have the "harmonious development of agriculture, industry, and commerce."[31] Maeda also adopted Tisserand's idea of "production" that had a strong mercantilist overtone in its emphasis of self-sufficiency and export promotion.[32]

Sydney Crawcour has speculated that Maeda may have read Friedrich List's *National System of Political Economy* translated into French by Henri Richelot of the French Ministry of Commerce in 1851.[33] This may well have been true. In Tisserand, at any rate, Maeda would have seen the implementation of Listian state activism in the promotion of industrial capacity.

Maeda echoed a Listian argument when he later wrote,

The rise to European preeminence of English commerce, German agriculture, French art, and Belgian industry was, if you look into their origins and history, in every case thanks to enlightened rulers and wise ministers. Such things have never arisen by mere chance.[34]

Here Maeda refuted the liberal view that economic development was best left undisturbed. The government, Maeda believed, had to take a leadership role in creating a modern capitalist economy. On this fundamental assumption, government officials in both Japan and the Western late developing nations agreed.

In terms of fundamental ideology, it is unlikely that Eugene Tisserand swayed Maeda very much. Maeda probably chose to study with Tisserand precisely because of their common economic nationalist views. As we have seen, economic nationalist thought in Satsuma already stressed the state's role in promoting the domain's wealth. In France, Maeda built upon this ideology through study of specific techniques of industrial promotion.

When Maeda returned to Japan, he supported Ōkubo's plan to establish a trading company to bypass foreign merchants. From his memorandum on the subject, we see a number of economic nationalist themes reiterated. His 1879 "A Partial Opinion on Direct Trade" (*Choku bōeki iken ippan*) called for a return of Japan's trading rights. If Japanese merchants displaced the foreigners in the control of trade, there would be much to be gained. This was to be a two-pronged strategy. First, develop Japanese trading companies to bypass foreign control of Japan's international trade. Second, assist businesses that were producing for export.[35]

This document on direct trade is most revealing of Maeda's ideological orientation.

> I hope that in all endeavors under heaven we can construct and implement a policy that is not based on empty theories, but rather on the actual condition of the people and is appropriate to the people's temperament and general attitude.
>
> I have put myself into the foreign trade marketplace and have earnestly examined conditions there. Since the opening of our ports, foreign merchants have exclusively held all of the trading rights and the pressure exerted on us year in and year out has been extreme. For this reason, there has been an imbalance of imports and exports and our specie has been flowing out at the high average rate of seven million yen per year.
>
> Now is the time to quickly secure the return of our commercial rights and radically change the dignity of our trade. Specie is becoming increasingly scarce, the value of paper currency is rapidly declining and prices are rising. The entire nation's energy is in a state of decay and in the midst of these unspeakable circumstances, it is no time for silence.[36]

Maeda's export promotion strategy had three components: the establishment of an "imperial bank," a trading company, and the organization of producers. The imperial bank would be founded with government assistance and would handle foreign exchange transactions for Japanese enterprises producing for export.[37]

On the trading company, Maeda suggested delegating the government's goals to private firms.

> I am not arguing to open a new trade company different from those that have operated thus far. Rather, select six or seven well-organized and willing companies, protect their foreign exchange and entrust them with the business of direct trade. Of course as business grows and production increases, there will need to be more, but for now select six or seven.[38]

In Maeda's proposal to establish a trade company, we can see the economic nationalist themes clearly. Policy needed to be based on actual conditions rather than theory. The Japanese should not pay for any service from foreigners that they could do for themselves. The government should find private businesses that are already successful and provide capital and technological assistance to help them become more competitive.

In 1880, Ōkuma and Itō submitted a proposal for the creation of the Ministry of Agriculture and Commerce (MAC). In it they recognized the need for the government to cut expenses by selling the model factories. They also proposed to streamline the bureaucracy by unifying all industrial promotion efforts in a single ministry. The Home Ministry's agricultural promotion and train station construction offices, the Finance Ministry's commerce office, and the construction encouragement office of the Construction Ministry were all abolished and their functions transferred to the Ministry of Agriculture and Commerce.[39]

After the sale of the model factories, MAC was established and carried on industrial promotion efforts on a smaller scale. The Agricultural Promotion Office (*Kannōkyoku*) set up small-scale experimental stations to transfer technology in sugar, tobacco, and tea production.[40]

With the establishment of MAC, industrial policy took a more indirect course trying to assist private businesses in improving their productive techniques to compete in the international market. There was some difference of opinion between MAC and the Dajōkan Central State Council. MAC bureaucrats understandably wanted to pursue more aggressive and direct industrial promotion ventures, but due to a lack of funding from the center, they were forced to prioritize and take a more indirect approach.[41]

Maeda Masana joined the new ministry and conducted a comprehensive survey of Japan's resources. He published the results of this survey together with his vision for future development in *Kōgyō iken* ("Opinion on the Encouragement of Enterprise").[42]

Maeda's approach to improving production was through education, experiment, regulation, information reporting, and encouragement. For education, he called for agricultural and silk schools, traveling instructors, agricultural libraries, and model factories. He advocated experimentation in the production of such products as silk, tea, sugar, and tobacco. Regulations would cover agricultural cooperatives and prevent silk worm blights and other diseases. Government bureaucrats would encourage industry through exhibitions of new techniques, opening "mutual progress societies," and establishing experimental and research stations.[43]

Maeda argued that the benefits of the pilot plants had little to do with the actual profits they generated.

> The improvement in quality of our raw silk and the progress we have made so far must be credited chiefly to government encouragement. Furthermore, the implementation of that encouragement was in the appropriate energy with which the factory in question [Tomioka Silk Filature] was constructed. But we need to make clear what that factory's operational purpose from the very beginning was. The temptation is to chafe over the losses in operation of this factory that cost so much money to start.
>
> However the purpose in starting this factory was to provide a model for the improvement of raw silk quality and not to make a profit in its operation. If this factory's silk made privately produced silk inferior, it would not succeed as a model. We must conclude that this improvement in quality must also include prominent private producers. We should not be concerned with whether or not government-built factories directly make a profit. It is absolutely clear that even operating at a loss year after year, silk produced at Tomioka has helped support the value of Japanese silk in the overseas market. Since this has indirectly assisted silk producers throughout Japan, we should conclude that its losses have been small while its benefits have been great.[44]

Maeda believed that Matsukata's reduction in state enterprises was unfortunate. He recognized that they operated at a loss, but argued that the government had a responsibility to bear these losses to help private producers become acclimated to the requirements of international trade. He justified his position by appealing to the state's moral duty to promote state power.

> Some say protection and others say freedom. Although in theory they are directly opposing views, they return to the same point. If protection is

suitable, there are advantages to it. Similarly, if freedom is inappropriate it can cause great damage. If there is an advantage, there should be intervention. If there is harm, we should not consider freedom. Why should we adhere absolutely to theory? English free trade or American protection is neither good nor bad. It is nothing more than a policy to protect things appropriate to that country's situation.

Since the Restoration, many have studied abroad and examined the situation overseas. But few have really noticed that country's conditions. Therefore, there is a tendency for those who return from England to want to import the English system and learn English ways and those who return from France to seek to implement French law and follow French style. They carelessly say this without giving the least thought to Japan's level.

In this way, when discussing lifestyles, they say we need European homes . . . On transportation, they say we need roads and waterways like they have in Europe. This is nothing more than using our limited capital to buy ornaments to display their wealth and beauty. Or they think that if we have roads, waterways, and railroads like they have in Europe and America, we will have wealth like they have in Europe and America. We should say they have been seduced. Well now, those who want to uselessly buy foreign goods to open the country do not go far enough. If we really are seeking things that will bring profit, we must carefully consider point by point the level of our people's knowledge, their standard of living, and how they engage in agriculture, manufacturing, and commerce. If we know our level well, we will understand what to do about secondary things like nice food and convenient transportation.[45]

The main thrust of Maeda's argument for the *Kōgyō iken* can be found here. This shows the influence of the historical economists who disparaged theory and argued for empirical research. Actual conditions, as interpreted by enlightened government officials, would dictate what policy should be adopted. Maeda's view of economic development also was holistic. It was not simply a matter of liberalism versus protectionism in trade. The entire national situation including military preparations, education, resource management, and quality of life had to be taken into consideration.[46]

In Maeda's *Kōgyō iken* we see the same economic nationalist themes that Satō Nobuhiro proposed to Satsuma sixty years earlier. The wise ruler should begin with a careful survey of his territory's resources. These resources not only included raw materials for industry, but also the people's abilities and morale was more important to the country's long-term success. A strategy could then be devised to import technology from abroad that was appropriate to actual conditions.

Conclusion

In the early 1880s, Godai Tomoatsu, Matsukata Masayoshi, and Maeda Masana each created their own variations of the economic development strategy that was articulated in Satsuma fifty years earlier. Godai emphasized the importance of trade in acquiring the specie that he believed a nation needed to be powerful and prosperous. His proposal called on the government to provide financial support for entrepreneurs involved in both import substitute and export industries.

Finance Minister Matsukata Masayoshi believed that self-reliance and the avoidance of debt should be the government's top priority and was willing to scale back direct industrial promotion. Matsukata's drive for self-sufficiency was reminiscent of Zusho Hirosato's 1830s Satsuma policy of financial contraction to maintain the domain's independence.

Maeda Masana, in his *Kōgyō iken* development plan, recalled the early *keisei saimin* argument that the ruler must do what was appropriate for conditions. Maeda believed that it was fine to strive for equality with the West, but government must start with the foundation that Japan already had in place. Japan had its unique history and it would be futile to ignore that heritage. In Maeda's view, the Japanese needed to focus first on improving traditional products such as silk, tea, rice, and pottery for export. With the profit from these goods, Japan could branch into Western-style industries over time.

Godai Tomoatsu, Matsukata Masayoshi, and Maeda Masana each illustrated a different facet of the economic nationalist *fukoku kyōhei* drive for self-sufficiency that Meiji leaders derived through synthesizing their observations of Western economic institutions with the strategic realism inherited from late Tokugawa era Satsuma. Although their specific policy recommendations differed somewhat, each had reached the conclusion that economic development was a process that the state could and should facilitate to reach the larger national goals of wealth and power.

Conclusion

By the 1890s, the Japanese government had established the most important institutions of capitalism. While scholars from the Anglo-American tradition have tended to emphasize what they regard as a high degree of Japanese state activism in the economy, we must remember that this applied only to those industries that were deemed strategically important to the military defense of the nation-state. Given the Tokugawa system's authoritarian nature, the Meiji leaders' commitment to market capitalism in most of Japan's economic activity is even more remarkable than its occasional intervention. This practical shift from the Tokugawa regime's tight state regulation of economic activity to one of relatively free markets in the Meiji era required a dramatic transformation of Japanese leaders' economic ideology.

Japan's ability to adapt relatively quickly to the growing pressures of the international market was largely the product of the late Tokugawa period's ideological legacy. Well before the United States forced the Japanese into a series of commercial treaties, domain officials and the intellectuals who served them had wrestled with an ideological system that seemed increasingly out of touch with reality. The Tokugawa peace of the previous 250 years had allowed commerce to flourish, but the samurai found it difficult to capture what they believed was their fair share of this wealth. Orthodox Confucian notions of order and propriety held that the samurai's moral superiority and selfless service earned them a privileged position while merchants' parasitic nature and greed put them at the bottom of society. By the late Tokugawa period, many samurai and even their daimyo leaders found themselves in debt to socially inferior merchants. This anomaly between the way things were theoretically supposed to be and the way they actually were forced some Japanese leaders and thinkers to work on reconciling their inherited ideology with the economic realities that they observed.

In this study, we have seen that Satsuma was one of several domains in the Tokugawa system that was in financial distress by the late

eighteenth century. Rising expenses associated with the alternate attendance system and the conspicuous consumption required to keep the
daimyo and domain officials in the proper trappings of their lofty station
put a severe drain on the domain treasury. The daimyo Shimazu
Shigehide's interest in Western books and science did not help matters as
the high expenses associated with these hobbies put additional strain on
the domain's budget. Revenue from rice had remained stable, but was
subject to fluctuation according to weather. By the early nineteenth century,
domain officials were looking more seriously at exploiting commercial
opportunities. The issue of the state's proper role in commercial activity
had long been the subject of vigorous debate in Confucian thought. The
debate over state monopolies of salt and iron that took place during the
Han Dynasty in 81 BC perhaps most famously illustrated the ideological
tension. State ministers in this case argued that the emperor was justified
in monopolizing these key commodities to pay for the defense of China's
frontier. Confucian scholars at the time disagreed. They argued that the
state's most important duty was to lead by moral example and asked how
the people could be expected to act virtuously when the state was engaged
in the greedy pursuit of profit. Although the scholars made a strong case,
economic forces proved decisive and the state monopolies persisted.

Perhaps the most important ideological change that accompanied the
advent of modernity was the transformation of the pursuit of profit from
a morally corrosive evil into the engine of innovation and progress. For
better or worse, some societies found this shift in their perceptions of
profit easier than others to make. The single most important factor in
determining the smoothness of the transition was whether the government of a country perceived the market as an ally in extending its power
and defending itself against foreign and domestic enemies.

As the Han salt and iron debate illustrated, the idea of government
monopolies was at odds with Confucian moral precepts. Of course, state
ministers could just dismiss the scholars' moral critique as simply out of
touch with the real world. Such a heavy-handed approach would have
needlessly alienated the intellectual elite who could, as a whole, be very
important in formulating the regime's ideological support. Instead we
see the state ministers rationalizing the state monopolies in the context
of the state's moral obligation to protect the people.

For centuries in the Confucian world, states' economic policies oscil-
lated between the poles of moralism and realism. In periods of social disorder, the morality of maintaining Confucian hierarchical principles was
emphasized. During times of financial crisis, the state's need to raise revenue through all possible means took precedence. In late Tokugawa

Japan, we see this issue play itself out on both ends of the spectrum. At the beginning of the period, the Tokugawa regime used Confucianism to establish its hegemony as the natural order. The Tokugawa were concerned with completing the process of pacification and unification that Oda Nobunaga and Toyotomi Hideyoshi had initiated. To this end, the bakufu established both institutional mechanisms of surveillance and control and ideological concepts of hierarchy and propriety. Merchant activity was recognized as a necessary evil, but the authorities attempted to strictly control it and keep merchants in their place at the bottom of the four-tiered class hierarchy. As commerce began to make merchants rich at the expense of the morally superior samurai, elite opinion shifted to a more utilitarian view of state involvement in commerce.

Perhaps the most important difference between the Chinese and Japanese cases was the fact that Japanese domain states found themselves in competition for prestige in the Tokugawa system and that competition soon became a competition for wealth. Chinese and Japanese Confucian responses to commerce reflected this difference in circumstances. Competition in the Japanese case led intellectuals to move beyond state monopolies to a broader conception of economic development as an important component in a state's larger strategy to stay in power.

Intellectuals and officials legitimated state involvement in commerce in the language of "ordering the realm and saving the people." How could domains help the people if they were bankrupt? The wise ruler, therefore, would have to give commerce greater emphasis than his predecessors had which, in turn, led to a growing identification of the ruler with the economic prosperity of his domain. This ideological realignment of the state official from moral exemplar and preserver of the status quo to promoter of economic development was gradual, but had a dramatic impact on Japan's historical trajectory.

This move toward strategic economic policies was coupled with an equally important philosophical shift regarding the nature of knowledge itself. To undermine the Neo-Confucian emphasis on natural principle and its implication that the Tokugawa hegemony was the natural order, philosophers turned to historical relativism. They argued that proper policy and action was dependent upon the particular characteristic of a historical moment. Tokugawa Ieyasu may have been a sage, but only because he established institutions that were appropriate to his particular time and place. If the Tokugawa order was not the product of enduring natural principles, it was only a matter of time until it would be replaced with a new set of institutions that were more appropriate to a new historical period.

As we have seen, *tozama* domains outside the shogun's direct control were particularly willing and able to pursue heterodox philosophy and commercial opportunity. Although the Tokugawa defeated these domains at Sekigahara, they were too large and powerful to be completely subjugated. Consequently, they enjoyed more freedom of action than the *fudai* or *shimpan* domains, but at the cost of exclusion from the bakufu positions. These domains' traditional enmity with the Tokugawa, their powerful size, and their geographic location on the periphery of the Tokugawa system gave leaders both the incentive and the means to increase their power and prestige relative to both the bakufu and other domains.

Satsuma is an important example of the transformation of a domain's ideological perceptions of commerce in the late Tokugawa period because several of the officials who helped create the institutions of Meiji Japanese capitalism came from this domain. Between 1800 and 1850, Satsuma followed a typical pattern of the state trying to monopolize key commodities to produce revenue to support the domain's rising expenses.

To do this, the domain sent officials to study with political economists who made their livings selling financial advice to daimyo. One of these political economists, Satō Nobuhiro, was especially influential. Satō visited Satsuma in 1786 and again in 1805. Between 1828 and 1830, he furnished Chief Officer Igai with copies of his *Keizai Teiyō*, *Nōsei Honron*, and *Satsuma Keii*. He advocated the thorough investigation of actual conditions and exploitation of Satsuma's particular climate and commercial advantages to advance the wealth of the domain's economy.

To implement the reforms Satō suggested, daimyo Shimazu Shigehide appointed Zusho Hirosato. Zusho simply repudiated the debts that the domain had accumulated with Osaka merchants over many years of chronic budget deficits. Unable to borrow more money, Zusho and Satsuma officials were forced to find new ways to finance its needs. Following policies similar to Satō's earlier suggestions, Zusho increased the production of Satsuma's existing sugar monopoly and encouraged domain merchants to explore the commercial potential of other commodities such as camphor and wax. These efforts proved successful and Satsuma emerged from the Tempō era financial crises with a budget surplus and a growing domain treasury.

Western ships seeking trade approached the Ryūkyū islands much earlier than Commodore Perry's famous mission. In fact, Satsuma had been circumventing the bakufu's control over foreign relations and trading with Western countries via the Ryūkyūs. In the 1840s the French attempted to conclude a formal commercial treaty with the Ryūkyū Kingdom and precipitated a crisis. Shimazu Nariakira was rightly concerned that Japan's continued policy of seclusion would be impossible without adequate military defense. This brought him into conflict with his father daimyo Shimazu Narioki and his adviser Zusho Hirosato. Zusho did not want the *han* treasury that he had struggled for nearly two decades to build up depleted through a rapid expansion of military expenditures. To get rid of Zusho, Nariakira divulged Satsuma's illicit trade through the Ryūkyūs to the bakufu officials. Zusho was forced to accept responsibility and committed suicide while Narioki had to accept early retirement.

Once in control as daimyo of Satsuma, Shimazu Nariakira responded to increasing Western pressure by promoting research into industries that could improve Satsuma's naval defenses. Takano Chōei was one of the chief intellectual influences on Nariakira's and Takano's recommendations of radical reform, and Western learning led Nariakira to change the curriculum of Satsuma education and establish an institute to experiment in Western science and technology. Perhaps Nariakira's most important legacy, however, was in the young talent that he encouraged and promoted. Under Nariakira's leadership future Meiji leaders such as Godai Tomoatsu, Ōkubo Toshimichi, Saigō Takamori, Matsukata Masayoshi, and Maeda Masana began their training. It is the continuity of personnel that presents the most promising avenue for understanding the influence of late Tokugawa ideology concerning the political economy on the early Meiji vision for industrial development.

It is important to remember, however, that this heritage is not deterministic, for each of these leaders would adopt a different approach to their shared goal of promoting the country's wealth and power. Ōkubo was perhaps closest to Nariakira's style of state-led industrial promotion. Godai Tomoatsu soon left government and became a private entrepreneur. Matsukata Masayoshi was persuaded by liberal economics if not politics and greatly reduced the range of economic activity that the government considered strategic. Maeda Masana quarreled with Matsukata on whether the government should first promote Western heavy industry or nurture traditional rural industries to form a foundation for later development. We see in this diversity of approaches even among leaders from the same domain that their Tokugawa era experience is not enough to explain their specific policy choices. These decisions had more to do with the politics of the moment in which they were made.

Nevertheless, the intellectual framework that these leaders used to interpret their environments did have roots in their earlier experience.

When traveling to the West, the Meiji leaders had to determine which elements of industrial capitalism were applicable to the Japanese case and which were culturally specific. Given the Tokugawa authoritarian heritage, we would expect a centrally controlled command economy in which the government is the main entrepreneur and distributor of resources. Ōkubo Toshimichi's "Promote production, encourage industry" campaign led by state-owned model factories was a clear example of this impulse for government control. Yet, when the government enterprises later proved to be too heavy a financial burden for the government to bear, a philosophical movement toward historical relativism allowed the adoption of liberal institutions when they were "appropriate to the trend of the times."

By 1885, the Meiji leaders, many of whom were from Satsuma, had firmly established capitalism as the ordering principle of the Japanese economy. Although the German Historical School would have a profound influence on the next generation of Japanese government leaders hoping to expand the government's role in the economy in the 1890s, the basic principles of capitalism were really never in dispute. Rather, later debates focused on ways that government intervention might help ameliorate the deleterious effects of capitalist competition rather than on any serious challenge to the principles of private property and the pursuit of profit.

Notes

Introduction

1. Thomas C. Smith, *Native Sources of Japanese Industrialization* (Berkeley: University of California Press, 1988), 135.
2. Chalmers Johnson, *MITI and the Japanese Miracle: The Growth of Industrial Policy* (Stanford: Stanford University Press, 1982).
3. Bai Gao, *Economic Ideology and Japanese Industrial Policy: Developmentalism from 1931 to 1965* (Cambridge: Cambridge University Press, 1997).
4. Noguchi Yukio, *1940 nen taisei* (Tokyo: Tōyō Shimpōsha, 1995).
5. Richard J. Samuels, *Rich Nation, Strong Army* (Ithaca: Cornell University Press, 1994).
6. William D. Wray, *Mitsubishi and the N.Y.K., 1870–1914: Business Strategy in the Japanese Shipping Industry* (Cambridge: Harvard University Press, 1984).
7. Takafusa Nakamura, *Economic Growth in Prewar Japan*, trans. Robert A. Feldman (New Haven: Yale University Press, 1983), 37.
8. Henry Rosovsky, "Japan's Transition to Modern Economic Growth, 1868–1885," in *Industrialization in Two Systems*, ed. Henry Rosovsky (New York: Wiley, 1966), 113.
9. E. Sydney Crawcour, "The Tokugawa Period and Japan's Preparation for Modern Economic Growth," *Journal of Japanese Studies* 1, no. 1 (1974), 117.
10. Thomas C. Smith, *Political Change and Industrial Development in Japan: Government Enterprise, 1868–1880* (Stanford: Stanford University Press, 1955), 12.
11. Tetsuo Najita, "Conceptual Consciousness in the Meiji Ishin," in *Meiji Ishin: Restoration and Revolution*, ed. Michio Nagai and Miguel Urritia (Tokyo: United Nations University Press, 1985), 92.
12. See, e.g., Sumiya Etsuji, *Nihon keizaigaku shi* (Tokyo: Minerubua Shobō, 1958) and Tsukatani Akihiro, *Kindai nihon keizai shisōshi kenkyū* (Tokyo: Kōbundō, 1960).
13. Sugihara Shirō, Sakasai Takahito, Fujiwara Akio, and Fujii Takashi, eds., *Nihon no keizai shisō yonhyakunen* (Tokyo: Nihon Keizai Hyōronsha, 1990).

14. Byron K. Marshall, *Capitalism and Nationalism in Prewar Japan: The Ideology of the Business Elite, 1868–1941* (Stanford: Stanford University Press, 1967), 46–47.

15. Fujita Teiichirō, *Kinsei keizai shisō no kenyū* (Tokyo: Yoshikawa Kōbunkan, 1966), 219.

16. Luke S. Roberts, *Mercantilism in a Japanese Domain* (Cambridge: Cambridge University Press, 1998), 28.

17. Institutional Economists have pointed out that one of the important contributions that governments can make to economic development is to create institutions that enforce property rights and reduce the costs of conducting economic transactions. See Douglass North, *Institutions, Institutional Change, and Economic Performance* (Cambridge: Cambridge University Press, 1990).

1   Confucian Statecraft and Ideological Innovation

1. On Hideyoshi's surveys and redistribution of holdings, see Mary Elizabeth Berry, *Hideyoshi* (Cambridge: Harvard University Press, 1982), 99–146.

2. For more information on daimyo classifications, see Harold Bolitho, *Treasures among Men* (New Haven, CT: Yale University Press, 1974), 44–47.

3. Confucius, *Analects*, trans D. C. Lau (London: Penguin Books, 1970), 74.

4. Mencius, *Mencius*, trans. D. C. Lau (London: Penguin Books, 1970), 49.

5. On the evolution of the notion in Japan that the ruler's interest was synonymous with the "public good" where subordinate's ambitions were "duplicitous private thoughts," see Mary Elizabeth Berry, "Public Peace and Private Attachment: The Goals and Conduct of Power in Early Modern Japan." *Journal of Japanese Studies* 12, no. 2 (1986): 237–71.

6. "The Debate on Salt and Iron," in *Chinese Civilization: A Sourcebook*, ed. Patricia Buckley Ebrey (New York: Free Press, 1993), 61. See also *Discourses on Salt and Iron: A Debate on State Control of Commerce and Industry in Ancient China*, trans. Esson M. Gale. (Taipei: Ch'eng Wen, 1973).

7. Xinzhong Yao, *An Introduction to Confucianism* (Cambridge: Cambridge University Press, 2000), 63–67, 105–08.

8. Masao Maruyama, *Studies in the Intellectual History of Tokugawa Japan*, trans. Mikiso Hane (Princeton: Princeton University Press, 1974), 16–17.

9. Hayashi Razan, "The Confucian Way," in *Sources of Japanese Tradition*, ed. Ryusaku Tsunoda, William Theodore De Bary, and Donald Keene, *Sources of Japanese Tradition Volume II* (New York: Columbia University Press, 1958), 348. For a sophisticated analysis of the Hayashi school of Tokugawa Neo-Confucianism, see Herman Ooms, *Tokugawa Ideology: Early Constructs, 1570–1680* (Princeton: Princeton University Press, 1985).

10. Kumazawa Banzan, "The Development and Distribution of Wealth," in *Sources of Japanese Tradition*, 379.

11. Kumazawa Banzan quoted in Tessa Morris-Suzuki, *A History of Japanese Economic Thought* (London: Routledge, 1989), 17.

12. Nakai Nobuhiko, and James L. McClain, "Commercial Change and Urban Growth in Early Modern Japan," in *Cambridge History of Japan, Volume Four: Early Modern Japan*, ed. John Whitney Hall (Cambridge: Cambridge University Press, 1991), 539.

13. Ibid., 545.

14. Susan Hanley, *Everyday Things in Premodern Japan* (Berkeley: University of California Press, 1997), 20–24.

15. Thomas C. Smith, *Native Sources of Japanese Industrialization* (Berkeley: University of California, 1988), 86–87.

16. Ibid., 91.

17. Thomas S. Kuhn, *The Structure of Scientific Revolutions* (Chicago: University of Chicago Press, 1962), 53.

18. The terms "fundamentalist" and "realist" in the context of late Tokugawa political thought can be found in Kenneth B. Pyle, *Making of Modern Japan* (Lexington, Ma: Heath, 1996), 53.

19. Description of Kyōhō reforms from Tsuji Tatsuya, "Politics in the Eighteenth Century," in *Cambridge History of Japan; Volume Four: Early Modern Japan*, 445–51. On the use of sumptuary laws to maintain social order, see Donald H. Shively, "Sumptuary Regulations and Status in Early Tokugawa Japan," *Harvard Journal of Asiatic Studies* 25 (1964–1965): 123–64.

20. Tetsuo Najita, "Conceptual Consciousness in the Meiji Ishin," in *Meiji Ishin: Restoration and Revolution*, ed. Michio Nagai and Miguel Urritia (Tokyo: United Nations University Press, 1985), 84–85.

21. Biographical information from "Ogyū Sorai," in Nagahara Keiji, ed., *Iwanami Nihonshi jiten* (Tokyo: Iwanami Shoten, 1999), 173.

22. On Sorai's criticism of Song Confucianism and his reinterpretation of the sage kings' importance, see Masao Maruyama, *Studies in the Intellectual History*, 92–102; Tetsuo Najita, "History and Nature in Eighteenth-Century Tokugawa Thought," in *Cambridge History of Japan; Volume Four: Early Modern Japan*, 602; and H. D. Harootunian, *Toward Restoration: The Growth of Political Consciousness in Tokugawa Japan* (Berkeley: University of California Press, 1970), 22–24.

23. Tetsuo Najita, "Political Economism in the Thought of Dazai Shundai (1680–1747)," *Journal of Asian Studies* 31, no. 4 (1972): 821–39, 823.

24. Dazai Shundai, "Keizairoku," in *Nihon shisō taikei 37: Sorai gakuha*, ed. Rai Tsutomu (Tokyo: Iwanami Shoten, 1972), 16.

25. Ibid., 17.

26. Ibid., 17–18.

27. For more on the Chinese Legalists, see Kung-chuan Hsiao, *A History of Chinese Political Thought*, trans. F. W. Mote, vol. 1 (Princeton: Princeton University Press, 1979), 397–408. On the interaction between Legalist concepts of wealth and power and Social Darwinism in late-nineteenth-century

China, see Benjamin Schwartz, *In Search of Wealth and Power* (Cambridge, MA: Belknap Press, 1964).

28. Dazai Shundai, "Keizairoku Shūi: Addendum to 'On the political economy,'" in *Tokugawa Political Writings*, ed. Tetsuo Najita (Cambridge: Cambridge University Press, 1998 [1730]), 143.
29. Ibid., 144.
30. Dazai, "Keizairoku," 20.
31. Nishikawa Shunsaku, and Amano Masatoshi, "Shohan no sangyō to keizai-seisaku," in *Kindai seichō no taidō*, ed. Shinbo Hiroshi and Saitō Osamu (Tokyo: Iwanami Shoten, 1989), 207.
32. Kaiho Seiryō, "Keikodan," in *Nihon shisō taikei 44: Honda Toshiaki Kaiho Seiryō*, ed. Tsukatani Akihiro and Kuranami Seiji (Tokyo: Iwanami Shoten, 1970), 222.
33. Kaiho, "Keikodan," 295.
34. Nakai Nobuhiko, and James L. McClain, "Commercial Change and Urban Growth in Early Modern Japan," in *Cambridge History of Japan; Volume Four: Early Modern Japan*, 589.
35. Tetsuo Najita, *Visions of Virtue in Tokugawa Japan* (Chicago: University of Chicago Press, 1987).
36. Luke S. Roberts, *Mercantilism in a Japanese Domain* (Cambridge: Cambridge University Press, 1998).
37. "Honda Toshiaki" in Nagahara Keiji, ed., *Iwanami Nihonshi jiten*, 1062.
38. Donald Keene, *The Japanese Discovery of Europe: Honda Toshiaki and Other Discoverers 1720–1798* (London: Routledge, 1952), 198.
39. Ibid., 176.
40. Najita, "Conceptual Consciousness," 92.

2 Confucian Moralism and Economic Realism in Satsuma

1. "Kyushu heitei" and "Satsuma han" in Nagahara Keiji, ed., *Iwanami Nihonshi jiten* (Tokyo: Iwanami Shoten, 1999), 306 and 494.
2. Haraguchi Torao, *Kagoshimaken no rekishi, Kenshi shirizu 46* (Tokyo: Yamakawa Shuppansha, 1973), 113–17.
3. "Satsuma yaki" in *Iwanami Nihonshi jiten*, 494.
4. Robert K. Sakai, "Feudal Society and Modern Leadership in Satsuma-han," *Journal of Asian Studies* 16 (1957), 365–76.
5. Ibid., 367.
6. Haraguchi, *Kagoshimaken no rekishi*, 176.
7. Sakai, "Feudal Society," 370.
8. Haraguchi, *Kagoshimaken no rekishi*, 160.
9. Sakai, "Feudal Society," 372.
10. Haraguchi, *Kagoshimaken no rekishi*, 158.

11. Sakai, "Feudal Society," 372.
12. Haraguchi, *Kagoshimaken no rekishi*, 148.
13. Robert K. Sakai, "The Satsuma-Ryūkyū Trade and the Tokugawa Seclusion Policy," *Journal of Asian Studies* 23, no. 3 (1964): 391–403, 391–92.
14. Haraguchi, *Kagoshimaken no rekishi*, 156.
15. Ronald P. Toby, *State and Diplomacy in Early Modern Japan* (Princeton: Princeton University Press, 1984), 182.
16. Sakai, "Satsuma-Ryūkyū Trade," 393.
17. Ibid., 395–96.
18. Ibid., 396–97.
19. Ibid., 397.
20. Ibid., 398.
21. Ibid., 400–02.
22. Haraguchi, *Kagoshimaken no rekishi*, 166–68.
23. Kanbashi Norimasa, *Shimazu Shigehide* (Tokyo: Yoshikawa kōbunkan, 1980), 18–20. "Muro Kyūsō" and "Riku yuengi taii," in *Iwanami Nihonshi jiten*, 1119, 1182.
24. "Tei Junsoku," in *Iwanami Nihonshi jiten*, 789.
25. Kanbashi, *Shimazu Shigehide*, 21.
26. "Kundō" quoted in Kanbashi, *Shimazu Shigehide*, 22.
27. Zhu Xi, "Preface to the *Great Learning* by Chapter and Phrase," in *Sources of Chinese Tradition*, ed. Wm. Theodore DeBary and Irene Bloom (New York: Columbia University Press, 1999), 722–23.
28. Ibid., 729.
29. Kanbashi, *Shimazu Shigehide*, 29.
30. "Hōreki chisui," *Iwanami Nihonshi jiten*, 1048.
31. *Shimazu rekidai ryakki*, (Kagoshima: Shimazu Kensho Kai, 1985), 135.
32. Ibid., 134–35.
33. Kanbashi, *Shimazu Shigehide*, 93–107, *Shimazu rekidai ryakki*, 133–34.
34. Kanbashi, *Shimazu Shigehide*, 24.
35. Matsui Masatō, *Satsuma hanshū Shimazu Shigehide* (Tokyo: Honpō shoseki, 1985), 127–31.
36. Ibid., 134–36.
37. *Shimazu rekidai ryakki*, 132.
38. Ibid., 136, Kanbashi, *Shimazu Shigehide*, 185–97.
39. Kanbashi, *Shimazu Shigehide*, 185–97.
40. "Satō Nohuhiro," in *Iwanami Nihonshi jiten*, 598.
41. Motoori Norinaga, "The True Tradition of the Sun Goddess," in *Sources of Japanese Tradition*, ed. Ryusaku Tsunoda, William Theodore De Bary, and Donald Keene, *Sources of Japanese Tradition Volume II* (New York: Columbia University Press, 1958), 18.
42. Hirata Atsutane, "The Land of the Gods," in *Sources of Japanese Tradition*, 39.
43. Satō Nobuhiro, "Confidential Memoir on Social Control," in *Sources of Japanese Tradition*, 71.

44. Satō Nobuhiro, "Keizai yōryaku," in *Nihon shisō taikei 45: Andō Shōeki Satō Nobuhiro*, ed. Bitō Masahide and Shimazaki Takao (Tokyo: Iwanami Shoten, 1977), 522.

45. Satō, "Confidential Memoir," 67–69.

46. Satō quoted in Tessa Morris-Suzuki, *A History of Japanese Economic Thought* (London: Routledge, 1989), 37.

47. Satō, "Confidential Memoir," 65.

48. I will be using Ryusaku Tsunoda's translation of the Japanese title, *Satsuma keii ki* as *How to Administer Satsuma*. However, it is interesting to note that *keii* has multiple meanings. In addition to "administration," Satō also uses it to mean longitude and latitude and takes great pains to establish Satsuma's geographic position. It can also mean length and breadth of a subject as well as the warp and weave of fabric that we saw in Dazai Shundai's earlier discussion of *keizai*.

49. Satō Nobuhiro, "Satsuma keii ki," in *Satō Nobuhiro kagaku zenshū*, ed. Shōichi Takimoto (Tokyo: Iwanami Shoten, 1926), 671.

50. Ibid., 679.

51. Ibid., 680.

52. Ibid.

53. Ibid.

54. Ibid., 683.

55. "Kyūrigaku," in *Iwanami Nihonshi jiten*.

56. Satō, "Satsuma keii ki," 685–86.

57. Ibid., 687.

3   Shimazu Nariakira and
Japan's First Industrial Policy

1. Although it is not entirely certain that Zusho had access to Satō Nobuhiro's treatise on Satsuma administration, Zusho's reforms were similar enough to those Satō had proposed to assume that he did. For a discussion of the empirical evidence for the connection between Satō Nobuhiro and Zusho Hirosato, see Haraguchi Torao, *Bakumatsu no Satsuma, Chūkō shinsho 101* (Tokyo: Chūō kōronsha, 1966), 72–75 and Kanbashi Norimasa, *Zusho Hirosato* (Tokyo: Yoshikawa kōbunkan, 1987), 79–80.

2. Harold Bolitho, "The Tempo Crisis," in *Cambridge History of Japan; Volume Five: The Nineteenth Century*, ed. Marius Jansen (Cambridge: Cambridge University Press, 1989), 118–22.

3. Ibid.

4. Ibid.

5. John Whitney Hall, *Japan: From Prehistory to Modern Times* (New York: Dell, 1971), 239.

6. Kanbashi, *Zusho Hirosato*, 74.

7. Haraguchi, *Bakumatsu no Satsuma*, 102.

8. Ibid.

9. Kanbashi, *Zusho Hirosato*, 90–91.

10. Ibid., 92.

11. Ibid.

12. Ibid., 98.

13. Tashiro Kazui, "Tokugawa jidai no bōeki, *Keizai shakai no seiritsu*, ed. Hayami Akira, Miyamoto Mataji, and Nihon keizai shi (Tokyo: Iwanami Shoten, 1988), 130–70, 161–64.

14. Ibid., 97–98.

15. Haraguchi, *Bakumatsu no Satsuma*, 112–19.

16. Ibid., 123.

17. Kanbashi, *Zusho Hirosato*, 114–15.

18. Ibid., 115–16.

19. Robert K. Sakai, "Shimazu Nariakira and the Emergence of National Leadership in Satsuma," in *Personality in Japanese History*, ed. Albert M. Craig and Donald H. Shively (Berkeley: University of California Press, 1970), 226–27.

20. Biographical information from Kanbashi Norimasa, *Shimazu Nariakira* (Tokyo: Yoshikawa Kōbunkan, 1993), 10–11.

21. Ibid., 17.

22. Ibid., 22–24.

23. Sakai, "Shimazu Nariakira and the Emergence of National Leadership in Satsuma," 211.

24. Ibid., 213.

25. This description of bakufu–Satsuma relations is adapted from Sakai, "Shimazu Nariakira and the Emergence of National Leadership in Satsuma."

26. Ibid., 217.

27. Kanbashi, *Shimazu Nariakira*.

28. Sakai, "Shimazu Nariakira and the Emergence of National Leadership in Satsuma," 225–27.

29. Ibid.

30. Kanbashi, *Shimazu Nariakira*, 25.

31. Biographical information compiled from "Takano Chōei," "Watanabe Kazan," and "Shiboruto" entries in Nagahara Keiji, ed., *Iwanami Nihonshi jiten* (Tokyo: Iwanami Shoten, 1999). For a more detailed biography, see Tsurumi Shunsuke, *Takano Chōei* (Tokyo: Asahi Shimbunsha, 1985).

32. See "Takano Chōei, "Bansha no goku," and "Watanabe Kazan" entries in *Iwanami Nihonshi jiten*.

33. Kanbashi, *Shimazu Nariakira*, 25–26.

34. Takano Chōei, "Yume monogatari," in *Nihon no meichō v. 25: Watanabe Kazan-Takano Chōei*, ed. Satō Shōsuke (Tokyo: Chūō kōronsha, 1972), 313.

35. Takano Chōei, "Kare wo shiri ichijo," in *Nihon no Meichō v. 25: Watanabe Kazan-Takano Chōei*, 355.
36. Ibid., 356.
37. On Chinese Legalist ideas of wealth and power, see Kung-chuan Hsiao, *A History of Chinese Political Thought*, trans. F. W. Mote, vol. 1 (Princeton: Princeton University Press, 1979), 393–97.
38. Kanbashi, *Shimazu Nariakira*, 93.
39. Ibid., 96–97.
40. For more detail on Nariakira's program, see *Kagoshima kenshi*, vol. 3 (Tokyo: Kintō Shuppansha, 1974), 243–78.
41. Robert K. Sakai, "Introduction of Western Culture to Satsuma," in *Report of the Second Kyushu International Cultural Conference*, ed. Kiyoshi Muto (Fukuoka: Fukuoka UNESCO Association, 1967), 28.
42. Shimazu Nariakira quoted in W. G. Beasley, *The Meiji Restoration* (Stanford: Stanford University Press, 1972), 121.
43. Sakai, "Introduction of Western Culture to Satsuma," 26.
44. W. G. Beasley, *Japan Encounters the Barbarian: Japanese Travellers in America and Europe* (New Haven, CT: Yale University Press, 1995), 50.
45. Mōri Toshihiko, *Ōkubo Toshimichi, Chūkō shinsho 190* (Tokyo: Chūō Kōronsha, 1969), 13–14.
46. Beasley, *Japan Encounters the Barbarian*, 49.
47. Nariakira quoted in Sakai, "Introduction of Western Culture to Satsuma," 27.
48. Ibid., 28.
49. Thomas C. Smith, *Native Sources of Japanese Industrialization* (Berkeley: University of California Press, 1988), 158.
50. Andō Yasushi, "Bakumatsu ishin Satsumahan no gōjū kyōiku," *Nihon rekishi*, no. 613 (1999): 1–18, 6–10.
51. Masakazu Iwata, *Ōkubo Toshimichi: The Bismark of Japan* (Berkeley: University of California Press, 1964), 31.
52. Haru Matsukata Reischauer, *Samurai and Silk: A Japanese and American Heritage* (Cambridge: Harvard University Press, 1986), 40–41.
53. Iwata, *Okubo Toshimichi*, 35.
54. William Davis Hoover, "Godai Tomoatsu (1836–1885): An Economic Statesman of Early Modern Japan" (Ph.D. Dissertation, University of Michigan, 1973).

4 Confucian and Capitalist Values in Conflict

1. For biographical information on Sakuma, see Richard Chang, *From Prejudice to Tolerance* (Tokyo: Sophia University, 1970), 101–10.
2. Sakuma quoted in Ibid., 152.

3. H. D. Harootunian, *Toward Restoration: The Growth of Political Consciousness in Tokugawa Japan* (Berkeley: University of California Press, 1970), 147.
4. Sakuma Shōzan, "Reflections on My Errors," in *Sources of Japanese Tradition*, ed. 105. Ryusaku Tsunoda, William Theodore De Bary, and Donald Keene, *Sources of Japanese Tradition Volume II* (New York: Columbia University Press, 1958), 105.
5. Ibid., 106.
6. Sakuma Shōzan, "Bakufu e bakusei kaikaku hihan," in *Nihon no meichō 30– Sakuma Shōzan, Yokoi Shōnan*, ed. Matsuura Ryō (Tokyo: Chūō Kōronsha, 1970), 277.
7. Ibid., 278.
8. Chang, *From Prejudice to Tolerance*, 162–63.
9. Sakuma quoted in Ibid., 162–63.
10. Chang, *From Prejudice to Tolerance*, 188.
11. Tessa Morris-Suzuki, *A History of Japanese Economic Thought* (London: Routledge, 1989), 38–43.
12. H. D. Harootunian, "Late Tokugawa Thought and Culture," in *Cambridge History of Japan, Volume Five: The Nineteenth Century*, ed. Marius Jansen (Cambridge: Cambridge University Press, 1989), 251.
13. Tamamuro Taijō, *Yokoi Shōnan* (Tokyo: Yoshikawa kōbunkan, 1967), 120.
14. Harootunian, "Late Tokugawa Thought and Culture," 247–50.
15. Harootunian, *Toward Restoration*, 328.
16. Yokoi Shōnan, "Kokuze sanron," in *Nihon no meichō 30– Sakuma Shōzan, Yokoi Shōnan*, 311.
17. Ibid., 312.
18. Ibid., 320.
19. Ibid., 326.
20. Ibid., 331.
21. Tamamuro, *Yokoi Shōnan*, 296–307.
22. Yūri Kimimasa, "Kinsatsu hakkō ni kansuru dajōkan fukoku," in *Keizai kōsō*, ed. Nakamura Masanori and Ishii Kanji, *Nihon kindai shisō taikei* (Tokyo: Iwanami Shoten, 1988), 5.
23. W. G. Beasley, *Japan Encounters the Barbarian: Japanese Travelers in America and Europe* (New Haven, CT: Yale University Press, 1995), 46–47.
24. Fujii Tetsuhiro, *Nagasaki kaigun denshūsho* (Tokyo: Chūō Kōronsha, 1991), 10–41.
25. Kunimitsu Shirō, "Godai Tomatsu," in *Shihonshugi no senkusha*, ed. Morikawa Hidemasa (Tokyo: TBS-Britannica, 1983), 88–89.
26. Ibid., 93–94.
27. William Davis Hoover, "Godai Tomoatsu (1836–1885): An Economic Statesman of Early Modern Japan" (Ph.D. Dissertation, University of Michigan, 1973), 36–42.
28. Masakazu Iwata, *Ōkubo Toshimichi: The Bismark of Japan* (Berkeley: University of California Press, 1964), 48.

29. Miyamoto Mataji, *Godai Tomoatsu den* (Tokyo: Yuhikaku, 1981), 7–11.

30. Marius Jansen, *Sakamoto Ryōma and the Meiji Restoration* (Princeton: Princeton University Press, 1961), 128–29.

31. Miyazawa Shinichi, *Satsuma to Igirisu no deai* (Kagoshima: Takagi Shobō Shuppan, 1987), 78.

32. Description of the incident drawn from Tokutomi Ichirō, *Kōshaku Matsukata Masayoshi den*, vol. 1 (Tokyo: Minyusha, 1935), 121–23 and Miyazawa, Chapter 5.

33. W. G. Beasley, "The Foreign Threat and the Opening of the Ports," in *Cambridge History of Japan, Volume Five: The Nineteenth Century*, 291–92.

34. Ibid.

35. Conrad Totman, *Collapse of the Tokugawa Bakufu, 1862–1868* (Honolulu: University of Hawaii Press, 1980), 14.

36. Haru Matsukata Reischauer, *Samurai and Silk: A Japanese and American Heritage* (Cambridge: Harvard University Press, 1986), 51.

37. Quoted in Mōri Toshihiko, *Ōkubo Toshimichi, Chūkō shinsho 190* (Tokyo: Chūō Kōronsha, 1969), 50.

38. Beasley, "Foreign Threat," 293.

39. Mōri, *Ōkubo Toshimichi*, 61.

40. Ibid.

41. Beasley, "Foreign Threat," 293.

42. For more information on the encounter at Namamugi and the Kagoshima bombardment, see *Kagoshima kenshi*, vol. 3 (Tokyo: Kintō Shuppansha, 1974), 190–208.

43. Iguro Yatarō, *Kuroda Kiyotaka* (Tokyo: Yoshikawa Kōbunkan, 1977), 6.

44. Mōri, *Ōkubo Toshimichi*, 80.

45. Tsuchiya Takao and Ōkubo Toshiaki, eds., *Godai Tomoatsu denki shiryō*, vol. 4 (Tokyo: Tōyō Keizai Shimpōsha, 1974), 26.

46. Hoover, "Godai Tomoatsu," 144–46.

47. Tsuchiya and Ōkubo, eds., *Godai Tomoatsu denki shiryō*, vol. 4, 33.

48. Ibid., 30.

49. Willy Vande Walle, "Le Comte des Charles de Montblanc (1833–1894), Agent for the Lord of Satsuma," in *Leaders and Leadership in Japan*, ed. Ian Neary (Richmond, Surrey: Japan Library, 1996), 39–41.

50. For more on Godai's trip, see *Kagoshima kenshi*, 212–42.

51. The text of the agreement can be found in Godai Ryūsaku, *Godai Tomoatsu den* (Tokyo: Shūkōsha, 1933), 38–42.

52. Vande Walle, "Le Comte des charles de Montblanc," 44–46.

53. Soda Osamu, *Maeda Masana* (Tokyo: Yoshikawa Kōbunkan, 1973), 9.

54. Soda, *Maeda Masana*, 27. Matsukata Masayoshi helped fund the publication of this dictionary. See Haru Matsukata Reischauer, *Samurai and Silk: A Japanese and American Heritage* (Cambridge: Harvard University Press, 1986), 68.

5 Satsuma Leaders and Early Meiji Capitalist Institutions

1. W. G. Beasley, *The Meiji Restoration* (Stanford: Stanford University Press, 1972), 241–42.
2. Beasley, *Meiji Restoration*, 287–88.
3. For a comprehensive narrative of the Meiji Restoration, see ibid., Chapter 11.
4. "Meiji Charter Oath," Ryusaku Tsunoda, William Theodore De Bary, and Donald Keene, eds. *Sources of Japanese Tradition Volume II* (New York: Columbia University Press, 1958), 136.
5. Katsuda Magoya, *Ōkubo Toshimichi den*, vol. 3 (Tokyo: Dōbunkan, 1911), 29.
6. Ibid., 48–49.
7. Kume Kunitake, *Beiō kairan jikki*, ed. Tanaka Akira, vol. 2 (Tokyo: Iwanami shoten, 1997), 83. Alternative translation in Kume Kunitake, *Iwakura Embassy, 1871–73*, ed. Tanaka Akira, trans. Graham Healey, vol. 2 (Tokyo: Iwanami Shoten, 2002), 74.
8. Ōkubo quoted in Albert Craig, "Kido Kōin and Ōkubo Toshimichi: A Psychohistorical Analysis," in *Personality in Japanese History*, ed. Albert Craig and Donald Shively (Berkeley: University of California Press, 1970), 296.
9. Katsuda, *Ōkubo Toshimichi den*, vol. 3, 51.
10. Ibid., 53.
11. Kume Kunitake, *Beiō kairan jikki*, ed. Tanaka Akira, vol. 3 (Tokyo: Iwanami Shoten, 1997), 298.
12. Ibid.
13. Ibid.
14. This description of Western economics texts is adapted from Sugihara Shirō, "Economists in Government: Ōkubo Toshimichi 'the Bismarck of Japan' and His Times," in *Enlightenment and Beyond: Political Economy Comes to Japan*, ed. Sugiyama Chūhei (Tokyo: Tokyo University Press, 1988), 211–12. On Ōshima's translation of List, see Nishida Taketoshi, *Ōshima Sadamasu: Hitō to gakusetsu*, ed. Takahashi Shoichirō, *Nihon no keizai gakusha* (Tokyo: Jitsugyō no Nihon sha, 1945).
15. Friedrich List, *National System of Political Economy*, trans. Sampson S. Lloyd, 1904 new edition (London: Longmans, Green, and Co., 1885). On the German Historical School, see Keith Tribe, *Strategies of Economic Order: German Economic Discourse 1750–1950* (Cambridge: Cambridge University Press, 1995), and Kenneth B. Pyle, "Advantages of Followership: German Economics and Japanese Bureaucrats, 1890–1925," *Journal of Japanese Studies* 1, no. 1 (1974).
16. Tessa Morris-Suzuki, *A History of Japanese Economic Thought* (London: Routledge, 1989), 54–55.
17. Ibid., 54
18. Sugiyama Chūhei, "Fukuzawa Yukichi," in *Enlightenment and Beyond: Political Economy Comes to Japan*, ed. Chūhei Sugiyama (Tokyo: Tokyo University Press, 1988), 53.

19. List, *National System* and Henry Charles Carey, *Principles of Political Economy* (New York: A.M. Kelley, 1965).
20. Sugiyama, "Fukuzawa Yukichi," 56.
21. Tokutomi Ichirō, *Kōshaku Matsukata Masayoshi den*, vol. 1 (Tokyo: Minyusha, 1935), 454.
22. Kanda Kōhei in Nakamura Masanori and Ishii Kanji, eds., *Keizai kōsō* (Tokyo: Iwanami Shoten, 1988), 136–41.
23. On the process of adoption of the Land Tax policy, see Kozo Yamamura, "The Meiji Land Tax Reform and its Effects," in *Japan in Transition: From Tokugawa to Meiji*, ed. Marius Jansen and Gilbert Rozman (Princeton, NJ: Princeton University Press, 1986).
24. The text of Matsukata's memorandum to Ōkubo can be found in Fujimura Tōru, ed., *Matsukata Masayoshi kankei monjo*, 18 vols., vol. 1 (Tokyo: Tōyō Kenkyūjo, 1979–1997), 278–80. Also in Tokutomi Ichirō, *Kōshaku Matsukata Masayoshi den*, vol. 1 (Tokyo: Minyusha, 1935), 504–09.
25. This description from Kozo Yamamura, "The Meiji Land Tax Reform and its Effects," 386.
26. Takahashi Kamekichi, *Nihon kindai keizai keiseishi*, 3 vols., vol. 2 (Tokyo: Tōyō keizai shinpōsha, 1968), 117.
27. Description of commutation from Marius Jansen, "The Ruling Class," in *Japan in Transition: From Tokugawa to Meiji*, 81.
28. Ōkuma Shegenobu in Nakamura Masanori and Ishii Kanji, eds., *Keizai kōsō*, 185.
29. On samurai military colonies, see Harry D. Harootunian, "The Economic Rehabilitation of the Samurai in the Early Meiji Period," *Journal of Asian Studies* 19, no. 4 (1960), 43 and Iguro Yatarō, *Kuroda Kiyotaka* (Tokyo: Yoshikawa Kōbunkan, 1977), 74.
30. For the Ōkubo–Saigō conflict, see Mark Ravina, *The Last Samurai* (Hoboken, NJ: Wiley, 2004), 188. For Kuroda's views, see Iguro Yatarō, *Kuroda Kiyotaka* (Tokyo: Yoshikawa Kōbunkan, 1977), 74–76.
31. Itō Hirobumi in Nakamura Masanori and Ishii Kanji, eds., *Keizai kōsō*, 9–10.
32. Ōkubo Toshimichi, "Shokusan kōgyō ni kansuru kengisho," in *Keizai kōsō*, 16–18.
33. Ibid.
34. Ibid.
35. Ibid.
36. List, *National System of Political Economy*.
37. For details on the Meiji government's specific industrial policy, see Thomas C. Smith, *Political Change and Industrial Development in Japan: Government Enterprise, 1868–1880*. (Stanford: Stanford University Press, 1955), 59–65.
38. Ibid., 59.
39. Ibid., 61–63.
40. Ibid., 64–65.

41. Sugihara Shirō, "Economists in Government," 221.
42. Morikawa Hidemasa, *Zaibatsu: The Rise and Fall of Family Enterprise Groups in Japan* (Tokyo: University of Tokyo Press, 1992), 12–15.
43. William D. Wray, *Mitsubishi and the N.Y.K., 1870–1914: Business Strategy in the Japanese Shipping Industry* (Cambridge: Harvard University Press, 1984), 153–54.
44. Ōkubo Toshimichi, "Chokuyūshutu kaisha setsuritsu no kengi," in *Keizai kōsō*, 42.
45. Ibid.
46. Ibid.
47. Ibid.
48. Ibid., 43.

6 Establishing a Firm Foundation for Economic Development

1. Stephen Vlastos, "Opposition Movements in Early Meiji, 1868–1885," in *Cambridge History of Japan Volume Five: The Nineteenth Century*, ed. Marius Jansen (Cambridge: Cambridge University Press, 1989), 426.
2. Henry Rosovsky, "Japan's Transition to Modern Economic Growth, 1868–1885," in *Industrialization in Two Systems*, ed. Rosovsky (New York: Wiley, 1966), 91–139, 134.
3. Rosovsky, "Japan's Transitiōn," 127–28.
4. Matsukata Masayoshi quoted in Thomas C. Smith, *Political Change and Industrial Development in Japan: Government Enterprise, 1868–1880*. (Stanford: Stanford University Press, 1955), 26.
5. Yamamoto Kakuma, *Yamamoto Kakuma kenpakusho* (Dōshisha Daigaku Gakujutsu Jōhō Senta Dōshisha Shiryōshitsu, 1869 [cited March 5, 2005]); available from http://duels.doshisha.ac.jp:88/denshika/yamamoto/128/imgidx128.html. For Yamamoto's connection to Matsukata see Yoshino Toshihiko, *Nihon ginkō shi*, vol.1 (Tokyo: Shunjusha, 1975), 46–48.
6. Tokutomi Ichirō, *Kōshaku Matsukata Masayoshi den*, vol. 1 (Tokyo: Minyusha, 1935), 697–702.
7. Rosovsky, "Japan's Transitiōn," 133–34.
8. Haru Matsukata Reischauer, *Samurai and Silk: A Japanese and American Heritage* (Cambridge: Harvard University Press, 1986), 38.
9. Matsukata Masayoshi, "Zaisei kaiki gairyaku," in *Nihon kindai shisō taikei 8: Keizai kōzō*, ed. Nakamura Masanori and Ishii Kanji (Tokyo: Iwanami Shoten, 1988), 96.
10. Matsukata Masayoshi, "Zaiseigi," in *Nihon kindai shisō taikei 8: Keizai kōzō*, 118.
11. Matsukata, "Zaisei kanki gairyaku," 97.
12. Ibid.

13. Ibid., 98–99.
14. Smith, *Political Change and Industrial Development in Japan*, 98–99.
15. Godai Tomoatsu, "Zaisei kyūji iken sho," in *Keizai kōsō*, 312–14.
16. Ibid., 316–18.
17. Ibid., 318–20.
18. Tsuchiya Takao and Ōkubo Toshiaki, eds., *Godai Tomoatsu denki shiryō*, vol. 4 (Tokyo: Tōyō Keizai Shimpōsha, 1974), 17–24.
19. On the sale of government enterprises, see Smith, *Political Change and Industrial Development in Japan*, 100.
20. Matsukata quoted in Tokutomi, *Kōshaku Matsukata*, 723–24.
21. Rosovsky, "Japan's Transitiōn," 136.
22. Matsukata Masayoshi, *Report on the Adoption of the Gold Standard* (Tokyo: Japanese Government Press, 1899), 50.
23. Ibid., 66.
24. On the influence of Meiji military expenditures on government finance, see Muroyama Yoshimasa, *Kindai nihon no gunji to zaiei* (Tokyo: Tokyo Daigaku Shuppankai, 1984). On bond issues, see Kamiyama Tsuneo, *Meiji keizai seisaku shi no kenkyū* (Tokyo: Kōshobō, 1995).
25. Kamiyama, *Meiji keizai seisaku*, 28–29.
26. Willy Vande Walle, "Le Comte des Charles de Montblanc (1833–1894), Agent for the Lord of Satsuma," in *Leaders and Leadership in Japan*, ed. Ian Neary (Richmond, Surrey: Japan Library, 1996), 51.
27. Ibid., 46–50.
28. Soda Osamu, *Maeda Masana* (Tokyo: Yoshikawa Kōbunkan, 1973), 44–45.
29. Ibid., 46–48.
30. Ibid., 49.
31. Ibid., 52.
32. Ibid., 52.
33. Sydney Crawcour, "Kōgyō iken: Maeda Masana and his View of Meiji Economic Development," *Journal of Japanese Studies* 23, no. 1 (1997), 104.
34. Maeda quoted in Ibid., 80–81.
35. Chō Yukio and Sumiya Mikio, eds., *Kindai Nihon keizai shisōshi I, Kindai Nihon shisō shi taikei* (Tokyo: Yūhikaku, 1969), 107.
36. Maeda Masana, "Kōgyō iken miteikō," in *Keizai kōsō*, ed. Nakamura Masanori and Ishii Kanji, *Nihon kindai shisō taikei* (Tokyo: Iwanami Shoten, 1988), 75.
37. Ibid., 78.
38. Ibid., 79.
39. Ōkuma Shigenobu and Itō Hirobumi, "Nōshōmushō setsuritsu no kengi," in *Keizai kōsō*, 102–04.
40. Kamiyama, *Meiji keizai seisaku*, 57.
41. Ibid., 58.
42. Maeda Masana, "Kōgyō iken," in *Kōgyō iken & shoken*, ed. Kondō Yasuo, *Meiji Taishō nōsei keizai meichōshū* (Tokyo: Nōsangyoson Bunka Kyōkai, 1975), 27–314.

43. Yoshikawa Hidezo, "Maeda Masana no shokusan kōgyō undō," *Dōshisha shōgaku* 14, no. 3–4 (1962), 61.
44. Maeda, "Kōgyō Iken," 310.
45. Ibid., 160–61.
46. Yoshikawa, "Maeda Masana," 56–57.

Glossary

Key Terms

bakufu	幕府	Shogun's government
bakumatsu	幕末	Later years of the Tokugawa period when domestic and foreign crises became acute
bansha no goku	蛮社の獄	1839 imprisonment of the "barbarian scholars" including Watanabe Kazan and Takano Chōei
Bansho Shirabesho	蛮書調所	Shogunate's Institute for the Study of Barbarian Books
bōeki rikkoku	貿易立国	Early Meiji slogan, "Build the country through trade"
bukken	物権	Rights to things or property rights
Choku bōeki iken ippan	直貿易意見一斑	Maeda Masana's 1879 proposal on direct trade
daimyo	大名	Semiautonomous regional lords
Dajōkan	太政官	Central state council in early Meiji period, replaced by Cabinet system in 1885
dōtoku giri	道徳義理	Moral obligation
fudai	譜代	Daimyo who were traditional vassals of the Tokugawa and were deemed more trustworthy
fukoku kyōhei	富国強兵	Rich country, strong military
fukyō	富強	Contraction of fukoku kyōhei often appearing in Meiji documents
fukyō wo itasu	富強を致す	Promote wealth and strength
gō	郷	Administrative district in Satsuma

gōnō	豪農	Peasants who accumulated wealth during the Tokugawa period and were an important source of entrepreneurial talent and capital
gōshi	郷士	Samurai assigned to rural districts
han	藩	Feudal domain
hensoku	変則	Different rules, irregular
ibutsu	異物	Something different
jisei	時勢	Trend of the times
jitsuryoku	実力	Practical effort
jōi	攘夷	Expel the barbarians
kaibutskan	開物館	Research institute in Satsuma
kaikoku	開国	Open country
kaikokuteki joi	開国的攘夷	Expel the barbarians by opening the country to gain knowledge and time
kan	貫	3.75 kilograms (8.72 pounds)
kanḡyō ryōkanin	官業寮官員	Official manager of state enterprise
keisei saimin	経世済民	Order the realm, save the people
keizai	経済	A contraction of *keisei saimin* that became the modern word for economics
Keizai yōryaku	経済要略	Satō Nobuhiro's outline of economics
kin	斤	600 grams (1.32 pounds)
Kinshiroku	近思録	Satsuma elders' report criticizing Shigehide's expenditures
kōan	公案	Zen conundrum designed to disable rational thought
kōbu gattai	公武合体	Union of court and shogunate
kogaku	古学	School of Ancient Learning that rejected Zhu Xi's and others' commentaries and favored direct exegesis of classical Chinese Confucian texts
Kōgyō iken	興業意見	Maeda Masana's 1884 development report
Kokinshū	古今集	Collection of waka poetry compiled in the tenth century
kokka	国家	State, literally, "national household"
kokken	国権	National rights or sovereignty
koku	石	4.96 bushels
kokueki	国益	National interest, profit, or advantage
kokugaku	国学	National Learning
kokushu	国主	National sovereign
konbu	昆布	Varieties of kelp
kundō	君道	Way of the Gentleman
kura yaku	蔵役	Official in charge of the storehouse or treasury
kyūrigaku	窮理学	Late Tokugawa and early Meiji period natural philosophy

Legalism	法家	School of thought in ancient China that rejected notion of leadership by moral example in favor of strong institutions, rewards, and punishments
minken	民権	Civil or popular rights
miso	味噌	Fermented soy bean paste
momme	匁	3.75 grams (0.1325 ounces)
okagemairi	御陰参り	Pilgrimages to Ise shrine
okonando	御小納戸	Official in charge of daimyo's diet, grooming, and household affairs
oyatoi gaikokujin	御雇い外国人	Foreign technicians hired in early Meiji era
ri	理	Principle
rōnin	浪人	Samurai without affiliation with a domain
ryō	両	Gold coin
sangi	参議	Senior councilor
san'yo	参与	Junior councilor
Satsuma yaki	薩摩焼	Pottery from Satsuma that became famous throughout Japan
sei	勢	Actual conditions
seppuku	切腹	Ritual suicide
shinpan	親藩	Daimyo who were relatives of the Tokugawa
Shintō	神道	Way of the gods
shishi	志士	Activists against the Tokugawa shogunate, often translated as "men of high purpose"
Satsuma keii ki	薩摩経緯記	Satō Nobuhiro's analysis of Satsuma's financial conditions
shō	升	1.8 liters (1.92 quarts)
shōchū	焼酎	Distilled alcoholic beverage
shōgun	将軍	Military ruler of Japan
shokusan kōgyō	殖産興業	Promote production, encourage enterprise
shoyūken	所有権	Right to derive benefits from and freely buy and sell property
Shu Jing	書經	Chinese *Book of Documents*
shūseikan	集成館	Satsuma research institute
tendō	天道	Way of Heaven
Tempō crisis	天保 crisis	1830s famine
waka	和歌	Several varieties of traditional Japanese poetry
yen	円	Japanese currency from Meiji era

za	座	Guilds granted monopoly rights by daimyo to produce and sell certain goods
zaibatsu	財閥	Financial and industrial conglomerates
Zaiseigi	財政義	Matsukata Masayoshi's 1880 principles of financial policy

Japanese Historical Periods

Warring States	戦国	1467–1568
Edo or Tokugawa	江戸 or 徳川	1600–1868
Genroku	元禄	1688–1704
Bunsei	文政	1818–1830
Tempō	天保	1830–1844
Meiji	明治	1868–1912

Chinese Historical Era

Spring and Autumn	春秋時代	722–481 BC
Warring States	戰國時代	5th century–221 BC
Qin Dynasty	秦朝	221–207 BC
Han Dynasty	漢朝	202 BC–AD 220
Tang	唐朝	618–907
Song	宋朝	960–1279
Yuan	元朝	1271–1368
Ming	明朝	1368–1644
Qing	清朝	1644–1911

Names and Places

Confucius	孔子	Chinese philosopher concerned with moral principles in human relationships and their contributions to an orderly society
Dazai Shudai	太宰春台	Ancient Studies scholar who advocated a realist approach to political economy to "order the realm and save the people"
Duke of Zhou	周公旦	Classical Chinese official who Confucius idealized as the ideal moral leader
Godai Tomoatsu	五代友厚	Led the first Satsuma mission abroad in 1865 and became an entrepreneurial leader in Osaka in the Meiji period
Han Feizi	韓非子	Chinese Legalist
Honda Toshiaki	本多利明	Studied Western mercantilist texts and advocated strategic development of economic resources

Kaiho Seiryō	海保青陵	Political economist
Kanda Kōhei	神田公平	Meiji official who drafted an important proposal for land tax reform
Li Si	李斯	Qin emperor's Legalist minister
Maeda Masana	前田正名	Meiji official who drafted a comprehensive report on economic development in 1884
Matsukata Masayoshi	松方正義	Minister of finance after 1881
Mencius	孟子	Major Confucian philosopher
Ogyū Sorai	荻生徂徠	Founder of Ancient Learning School that provided an alternative intellectual framework to Tokugawa Zhu Xi Confucianism
Ōkubo Toshimichi	大久保利通	Leader of the Meiji Restoration and main proponent of rapid industrialization
Ōkuma Shigenobu	大隈重信	Meiji Leader from Hizen who served as Finance Minister in the 1870s and was forced out the oligarchy in 1881 for his support of the liberal Popular Rights Movement
Saigō Takamori	西郷隆盛	Satsuma leader of the Meiji Restoration forces who later rebelled against the new regime's treatment of the samurai class
Satō Nobuhiro	佐藤信淵	Political economist who drafted an early economic development plan for Satsuma
Shen Buhai	申不害	Chinese Legalist state minister
Shimazu Hisamitsu	島津久光	Served as regent when his son Tadayoshi became daimyo of Satsuma
Shimazu Nariakira	島津斉彬	Progressive Satsuma daimyo who mentored many later leaders of the Restoration
Shimazu Shigehide	島津重豪	First Satsuma daimyo to seriously engage in Western learning
Shimazu Tadayoshi	島津忠義	Last daimyo of Satsuma
Tokugawa Ieyasu	徳川家康	First Tokugawa shogun
Wang Yangming	王陽明	Ming Confucian scholar who emphasized subjective intuition over rational thought
Yao, Shun, Yu	堯、舜、禹	Ancient Chinese sage kings.
Zhu Xi	朱熹	1130–1200, Chinese scholar closely associated with Neo-Confucian revival
Zusho Hirosato	調所広郷	Satsuma official in charge of domain economic reforms in the 1830s

Bibliography

Andō Yasushi. "Bakumatsu ishin Satsumahan no gōjū kyōiku." *Nihon rekishi*, no. 613 (1999): 1–18.

Banno Junji. " 'Fukoku' ron no seijishiteki kōsai." In *Matsukata zaisei to shokusan kōgyō*, edited by Umemura Mataji and Nakamura Takafusa, 37–52. Tokyo: Kokusai Rengō Daigaku, 1983.

Beasley, W. G. "The Foreign Threat and the Opening of the Ports." In *Cambridge History of Japan, Volume Five: The Nineteenth Century*, edited by Marius Jansen, 259–307. Cambridge: Cambridge University Press, 1989.

———. *Japan Encounters the Barbarian: Japanese Travellers in America and Europe*. New Haven, CT: Yale University Press, 1995.

———. *The Meiji Restoration*. Stanford: Stanford University Press, 1972.

Berry, Mary Elizabeth. *Hideyoshi*. Cambridge, MA: Harvard University Press, 1982.

———. "Public Peace and Private Attachment: The Goals and Conduct of Power in Early Modern Japan." *Journal of Japanese Studies* 12, no. 2 (1986): 237–71.

Bolitho, Harold. "The Tempo Crisis." In *Cambridge History of Japan, Volume 5: The Nineteenth Century*, edited by Marius Jansen, 116–67. Cambridge: Cambridge University Press, 1989.

———. *Treasures among Men*. New Haven, CT: Yale University Press, 1974.

Carey, Henry Charles. *Principles of Political Economy*. New York: A.M. Kelley, 1965.

Chang, Richard. *From Prejudice to Tolerance*. Tokyo: Sophia University, 1970.

Confucius. *Analects*. Translated by D. C. Lau. London: Penguin Books, 1979.

Craig, Albert. "Kido Kōin and Ōkubo Toshimichi: A Psychohistorical Analysis." In *Personality in Japanese History*, edited by Albert Craig and Donald Shively. Berkeley: University of California Press, 1970.

Crawcour, E. Sydney. "The Tokugawa Period and Japan's Preparation for Modern Economic Growth." *Journal of Japanese Studies* 1, no. 1 (1974): 113–25.

Crawcour, Sydney. "Kōgyō iken: Maeda Masana and His View of Meiji Economic Development." *Journal of Japanese Studies* 23, no. 1 (1997): 69–104.

Dazai Shundai. "Keizairoku Shūi: Addendum to 'On the political economy.' " In *Tokugawa Political Writings*, edited by Tetsuo Najita, 141–53. Cambridge: Cambridge University Press, 1998 [1730].

"The Debate on Salt and Iron." In *Chinese Civilization: A Sourcebook*, edited by Patricia Buckley Ebrey, 60–63. New York: Free Press, 1993.

Discourses on Salt and Iron: A Debate on State Control of Commerce and Industry in Ancient China. Translated by Esson M. Gale. Taipei: Ch'eng Wen, 1973.

Fujii Tetsuhiro. *Nagasaki kaigun denshūsho*. Tokyo: Chūō Kōronsha, 1991.

Fujimura Tōru. *Matsukata Masayoshi*. Tokyo: Nihon Keizai Shimbunsha, 1966.

———, ed. *Matsukata Masayoshi kankei monjo*. 18 vols. Tokyo: Tōyō Kenkyūjo, 1979–1997.

Fujita Teiichirō. *Kinsei keizai shisō no kenyū*. Tokyo: Yoshikawa Kōbunkan, 1966.

———. *Kokueki shisō no keifu to tenkai*. Osaka: Seibundō Shuppan, 1998.

Gao, Bai. *Economic Ideology and Japanese Industrial Policy: Developmentalism from 1931 to 1965*. Cambridge: Cambridge University Press, 1997.

Godai Ryūsaku. *Godai Tomoatsu den*. Tokyo: Shūkōsha, 1933.

Godai Tomoatsu. "Zaisei kyūji iken sho." In *Keizai kōsō*, edited by Nakamura Masanori and Ishii Kanji, 312–24. Tokyo: Iwanami Shoten, 1988.

Hall, John Whitney. *Japan: From Prehistory to Modern Times*. New York: Dell, 1971.

Hanley, Susan. *Everyday Things in Premodern Japan*. Berkeley: University of California Press, 1997.

Haraguchi Torao. *Bakumatsu no Satsuma, Chūkō shinsho 101*. Tokyo: Chūō Kōronsha, 1966.

———. *Kagoshimaken no rekishi, Kenshi shirizu 46*. Tokyo: Yamakawa Shuppansha, 1973.

Harootunian, H. D. "Late Tokugawa Thought and Culture." In *Cambridge History of Japan, Volume Five: The Nineteenth Century*, edited by Marius Jansen, 168–258. Cambridge: Cambridge University Press, 1989.

———. *Toward Restoration: The Growth of Political Consciousness in Tokugawa Japan*. Berkeley: University of California Press, 1970.

Harootunian, Harry D. "The Economic Rehabilitation of the Samurai in the Early Meiji Period." *Journal of Asian Studies* 19, no. 4 (1960): 433–44.

Hayashi Razan. "The Confucian Way." In *Sources of Japanese Tradition Volume II*, edited by Tsunoda, Ryusaku, William Theodore De Bary, and Donald Keene. New York: Columbia University Press, 1958, 348.

Hirata Atsutane. "The Land of the Gods." In *Sources of Japanese Tradition Volume II*, edited by Tsunoda, Ryusaku, William Theodore De Bary, and Donald Keene. New York: Columbia University Press, 1958, 39.

Hoover, William Davis. "Godai Tomoatsu (1836–1885): An Economic Statesman of Early Modern Japan." Ph.D. Dissertation, University of Michigan, 1973.

Howell, David L. *Capitalism from Within: Economy, Society, and the State in a Japanese Fishery*. Berkeley: University of California Press, 1995.

Hsiao, Kung-chuan. *A History of Chinese Political Thought*. Translated by F. W. Mote. Vol. 1. Princeton: Princeton University Press, 1979.

Iguro Yatarō. *Kuroda Kiyotaka*. Tokyo: Yoshikawa Kōbunkan, 1977.

Inukai, Ichiro. *Japan's First Development Strategy for Economic Development with Selected Translation of Kogyo Iken*. Edited by Watanabe Shinichi, *Policies for Socioeconomic Development of Japan*. Niigata: International University of Japan-International Development Program Press, 2003.

Iwahashi Masaru. *Kinsei Ninhon bukkashi no kenkyū*. Tokyo: Ōhara Shinseisha, 1981.

Iwata, Masakazu. *Ōkubo Toshimichi: The Bismark of Japan*. Berkeley: University of California Press, 1964.

Jansen, Marius. *Sakamoto Ryōma and the Meiji Restoration*. Princeton: Princeton University Press, 1961.

Johnson, Chalmers. *MITI and the Japanese Miracle: The Growth of Industrial Policy*. Stanford: Stanford University Press, 1982.

Kagoshima kenshi. Tokyo: Kintō Shuppansha, 1974.

Kaiho Seiryō. "Keikodan." In *Nihon shisō taikei 44: Honda Toshiaki Kaiho Seiryō*, edited by Tsukatani Akihiro and Kuranami Seiji. Tokyo: Iwanami Shoten, 1970.

Kamiyama Tsuneo. *Meiji keizai seisaku shi no kenkyū*. Tokyo: Kōshobō, 1995.

Kanbashi Norimasa. *Shimazu Nariakira*. Tokyo: Yoshikawa Kōbunkan, 1993.

———. *Shimazu Shigehide*. Tokyo: Yoshikawa Kōbunkan, 1980.

———. *Zusho Hirosato*. Tokyo: Yoshikawa Kōbunkan, 1987.

Katsuda Magoya. *Ōkubo Toshimichi den*. Tokyo: Dōbunkan, 1911.

Keene, Donald. *The Japanese Discovery of Europe: Honda Toshiaki and Other Discoverers 1720–1798*. London: Routledge, 1952.

Kuhn, Thomas S. *The Structure of Scientific Revolutions*. Chicago: University of Chicago Press, 1962.

Kumazawa Banzan. "The Development and Distribution of Wealth." In *Sources of Japanese Tradition Volume II*, edited by Tsunoda, Ryusaku, William Theodore De Bary, and Donald Keene, 379. New York: Columbia University Press, 1958.

Kume Kunitake. *Beiō kairan jikki*. Edited by Tanaka Akira. Tokyo: Iwanami Shoten, 1997.

———. *Iwakura Embassy, 1871–73*. Translated by Graham Healey. Edited by Tanaka Akira. Vol. 2. Tokyo: Iwanami Shoten, 2002.

Kunimitsu Shirō. "Godai Tomatsu." In *Shihonshugi no senkusha*, edited by Morikawa Hidemasa. Tokyo: TBS-Britannica, 1983.

List, Friedrich. *National System of Political Economy*. Translated by Sampson S. Lloyd. 1904 new edition, London: Longmans, Green, and Co., 1885.

Maeda Masana. "Kōgyō iken." In *Kōgyō iken & shoken*, edited by Kondō Yasuo, 27–314. Tokyo: Nōsangyoson Bunka Kyōkai, 1975.

Marshall, Byron K. *Capitalism and Nationalism in Prewar Japan: The Ideology of the Business Elite, 1868–1941*. Stanford: Stanford University Press, 1967.

Maruyama, Masao. *Studies in the Intellectual History of Tokugawa Japan*. Translated by Mikiso Hane. Princeton: Princeton University Press, 1974.

Matsui Masatō. *Satsuma hanshū Shimazu Shigehide*. Tokyo: Honpō Shoseki, 1985.

Matsukata Masayoshi. "Kaikanzei kaishōgi dai ichi." In *Meiji zenki zaisei keizai shiryō shūsei*, edited by Ōkurashō, 357–61. Tokyo: Kaizōsha, 1931.

———. *Report on the Adoption of the Gold Standard.* Tokyo: Japanese Government Press, 1899.

———. "Zaisei kaiki gairyaku." In *Nihon kindai shisō taikei 8: Keizai kōzō*, edited by Nakamura Masanori and Ishii Kanji, 96–102. Tokyo: Iwanami Shoten, 1988.

———. "Zaiseigi." In *Nihon kindai shisō taikei 8: Keizai kōzō*, edited by Nakamura Masanori and Ishii Kanji, 108–19. Tokyo: Iwanami Shoten, 1988.

Mencius. *Mencius.* Translated by D. C. Lau. London: Penguin Books, 1970.

Miyamoto Mataji. *Godai Tomoatsu den.* Tokyo: Yuhikaku, 1981.

Miyazawa Shinichi. *Satsuma to Igirisu no deai.* Kagoshima: Takagi Shobō Shuppan, 1987.

Morikawa Hidemasa. *Zaibatsu: The Rise and Fall of Family Enterprise Groups in Japan.* Tokyo: University of Tokyo Press, 1992.

Morris-Suzuki, Tessa. *A History of Japanese Economic Thought.* London: Routledge, 1989.

Motoori Norinaga. "The True Tradition of the Sun Goddess." In *Sources of Japanese Tradition Volume II*, edited by Tsunoda, Ryusaku, William Theodore De Bary, and Donald Keene. New York: Columbia University Press, 1958, 15–18.

Muroyama Yoshimasa. *Kindai Nihon no gunji to zaiei.* Tokyo: Tokyo Daigaku Shuppankai, 1984.

Nagahara Keiji, ed. *Iwanami Nihonshi jiten.* Tokyo: Iwanami Shoten, 1999.

Najita, Tetsuo. "Conceptual Consciousness in the Meiji Ishin." In *Meiji Ishin: Restoration and Revolution*, edited by Michio Nagai and Miguel Urritia. Tokyo: United Nations University Press, 1985.

———. "History and Nature in Eighteenth-century Tokugawa Thought." In *Cambridge History of Japan, Volume 4: Early Modern Japan*, edited by John Whitney Hall, 596–659. Cambridge: Cambridge University Press, 1991.

———. "Political Economism in the Thought of Dazai Shundai (1680–1747)." *Journal of Asian Studies* 31, no. 4 (1972): 821–39.

———. *Visions of Virtue in Tokugawa Japan.* Chicago: University of Chicago Press, 1987.

Nakai Nobuhiko and James L. McClain. "Commercial Change and Urban Growth in Early Modern Japan." In *Cambridge History of Japan, Volume 4: Early Modern Japan*, edited by John Whitney Hall, 519–94. Cambridge: Cambridge University Press, 1991.

Nakamura Masanori and Ishii Kanji, eds. *Keizai kōsō.* Tokyo: Iwanami Shoten, 1988.

Nakamura, Takafusa. *Economic Growth in Prewar Japan.* Translated by Robert A. Feldman. New Haven, CT: Yale University Press, 1983.

Nakamura Takafusa. "Meiji isshin shinki zaisei kinyū seisaku tenbō." In *Matsukata zaisei to shokusan kōgyō*, edited by Umemura Mataji and Nakamura Takafusa, 3–34. Tokyo: Kokusai Rengō Daigaku, 1983.

Nishida Taketoshi. *Ōshima Sadamasu: hito to gakusetsu.* Edited by Takahashi Shoichirō, *Nihon no keizai gakusha.* Tokyo: Jitsugyō no Nihon Sha, 1945.

Nishikawa Shunsaku and Amano Masatoshi. "Shohan no sangyō to keizai-seisaku." In *Kindai seichō no taidō,* edited by Shinbo Hiroshi and Saitō Osamu. Tokyo: Iwanami Shoten, 1989.

Noguchi Yukio. *1940 nen taisei.* Tokyo: Tōyō shimpōsha, 1995.

North, Douglass. *Institutions, Institutional Change, and Economic Performance.* Cambridge: Cambridge University Press, 1990.

Ōkubo Toshimichi. "Chokuyūshutu kaisha setsuritsu no kengi." In *Keizai kōsō,* edited by Nakamura Masanori and Ishii Kanji, 40–44. Tokyo: Iwanami Shoten, 1988.

———. "Shokusan kōgyō ni kansuru kengisho." In *Keizai kōsō,* edited by Nakamura Masanori and Ishii Kanji, 16–19. Tokyo: Iwanami Shoten, 1988.

Ōkuma Shigenobu and Itō Hirobumi. "Nōshōmushō setsuritsu no kengi." In *Keizai kōsō,* edited by Nakamura Masanori and Ishii Kanji, 102–04. Tokyo: Iwanami Shoten, 1988.

Ooms, Herman. *Tokugawa Ideology: Early Constructs, 1570–1680.* Princeton: Princeton University Press, 1985.

Pyle, Kenneth B. "Advantages of Followership: German Economics and Japanese Bureaucrats, 1890–1925." *Journal of Japanese Studies* 1, no. 1 (1974): 127–64.

———. *Making of Modern Japan.* Lexington, MA: Heath, 1996.

Ravina, Mark. *The Last Samurai.* Hoboken, NJ: Wiley, 2004.

Reischauer, Haru Matsukata. *Samurai and Silk: A Japanese and American Heritage.* Cambridge, MA: Harvard University Press, 1986.

Roberts, Luke S. *Mercantilism in a Japanese Domain.* Cambridge: Cambridge University Press, 1998.

Rosovsky, Henry. "Japan's Transition to Modern Economic Growth, 1868–1885." In *Industrialization in Two Systems,* edited by Henry Rosovsky, 91–139. New York: Wiley, 1966.

Sakai, Robert K. "Feudal Society and Modern Leadership in Satsuma-han." *Journal of Asian Studies* 16 (1957): 365–76.

———. "An Introductory Analysis." In *The Status System and Social Organization of Satsuma,* edited by Torao Haraguchi and Robert K. Sakai, 3–42. Honolulu: University of Hawaii, 1975.

———. "The Satsuma-Ryukyu Trade and the Tokugawa Seclusion Policy." *Journal of Asian Studies* 23, no. 3 (1964): 391–403.

———. "Shimazu Nariakira and the Emergence of National Leadership in Satsuma." In *Personality in Japanese History,* edited by Albert M. Craig and Donald H. Shively. Berkeley: University of California Press, 1970.

Sakuma Shōzan. "Bakufu e bakusei kaikaku hihan." In *Nihon no meichō 30-Sakuma Shōzan, Yokoi Shōnan,* edited by Matsuura Ryō, 259–78. Tokyo: Chūō Kōronsha, 1970.

———. "Reflections on My Errors." In *Sources of Japanese Tradition,* edited by Tsunoda, Ryusaku, William Theodore De Bary, and Donald Keene New York: Columbia University Press, 1958, 101–09.

Samuels, Richard J. *Rich Nation, Strong Army*. Ithaca: Cornell University Press, 1994.

Satō Nobuhiro. "Confidential Memoir on Social Control." In *Sources of Japanese Tradition*, edited by Tsunoda, Ryusaku, William Theodore De Bary, and Donald Keene. New York: Columbia University Press, 1958, 67–69.

———. "Keizai yōryaku." In *Nihon shisō taikei 45: Andō Shōeki Satō Nobuhiro*, edited by Bitō Masahide and Shimazaki Takao. Tokyo: Iwanami Shoten, 1977.

———. "Satsuma keii ki." In *Satō Nobuhiro kagaku zenshū*, edited by Shōichi Takimoto, 671–704. Tokyo: Iwanami Shoten, 1926.

Schwartz, Benjamin. *In Search of Wealth and Power*. Cambridge, MA: Belknap Press, 1964.

Shimazu rekidai ryakki. Kagoshima: Shimazu Kensho Kai, 1985.

Shively, Donald H. "Sumptuary Regulations and Status in Early Tokugawa Japan." *Harvard Journal of Asiatic Studies* 25(1964–1965): 123–64.

Smith, Thomas C. *Native Sources of Japanese Industrialization*. Berkeley: University of California, 1988.

———. *Political Change and Industrial Development in Japan: Government Enterprise, 1868–1880*. Stanford: Stanford University Press, 1955.

Soda Osamu. *Maeda Masana*. Tokyo: Yoshikawa Kōbunkan, 1973.

Sugihara Shirō. "Economists in Government: Ōkubo Toshimichi 'the Bismarck of Japan' and His Times." In *Enlightenment and Beyond: Political Economy Comes to Japan*, edited by Sugiyama Chūhei, 211–21. Tokyo: Tokyo University Press, 1988.

Sugihara Shirō, Sakasai Takahito, Fujiwara Akio, and Fujii Takashi, eds. *Nihon no keizai shisō yonhyakunen*. Tokyo: Nihon Keizai Hyōronsha, 1990.

Sugiyama Chūhei. "Fukuzawa Yukichi." In *Enlightenment and Beyond: Political Economy Comes to Japan*, edited by Chūhei Sugiyama, 37–58. Tokyo: Tokyo University Press, 1988.

Sumiya Etsuji. *Nihon keizaigaku shi*. Tokyo: Minerubua Shobō, 1958.

Takahashi Kamekichi. *Nihon kindai keizai hatatsushi*. 3 vols. Tokyo: Tōyō Keizai Shinpōsha, 1973.

Takano Chōei. "Kare wo shiri ichijo." In *Nihon no meichō v. 25: Watanabe Kazan—Takano Chōei*, edited by Satō Shōsuke, 352–68. Tokyo: Chūō Kōronsha, 1972.

———. "Yume monogatari." In *Nihon no Meichō v. 25: Watanabe Kazan—Takano Chōei*, edited by Satō Shōsuke, 313–21. Tokyo: Chūō Kōronsha, 1972.

Tamamuro Taijō. *Yokoi Shōnan*. Tokyo: Yoshikawa Kōbunkan, 1967.

Tashiro Kazui. "Tokugawa jidai no bōeki." In *Keizai shakai no seiritsu*, edited by Hayami Akira and Miyamoto Mataji, 130–70. Tokyo: Iwanami Shoten, 1988.

Toby, Ronald P. *State and Diplomacy in Early Modern Japan*. Princeton: Princeton University Press, 1984.

Tokutomi Ichirō. *Kōshaku Matsukata Masayoshi den*. Tokyo: Minyūsha, 1935.

Totman, Conrad. *Collapse of the Tokugawa Bakufu, 1862–1868*. Honolulu: University of Hawaii Press, 1980.

Tribe, Keith. *Strategies of Economic Order: German Economic Discourse 1750–1950*. Cambridge: Cambridge University Press, 1995.

Tsuchiya Takao and Ōkubo Toshiaki, eds. *Godai Tomoatsu denki shiryō*. Tokyo: Tōyō Keizai Shimpōsha, 1974.

Tsuji Tatsuya. "Politics in the Eighteenth Century." In *Cambridge History of Japan, Volume four: Early Modern Japan*, edited by John Whitney Hall, 425–77. Cambridge: Cambridge University Press, 1991.

Tsukatani Akihiro. *Kindai nihon keizai shisōshi kenkyū*. Tokyo: Kōbundō, 1960.

Tsunoda, Ryusaku, ed. *Sources of Japanese Tradition Volume II*. New York: Columbia University Press, 1958.

Tsurumi Shunsuke. *Takano Chōei*. Tokyo: Asahi Shimbunsha, 1985.

Vande Walle, Willy. "Le Comte des Charles de Montblanc (1833–1894), Agent for the Lord of Satsuma." In *Leaders and Leadership in Japan*, edited by Ian Neary. Richmond, Surrey: Japan Library, 1996.

Vlastos, Stephen. "Opposition Movements in Early Meiji, 1868–1885." In *Cambridge History of Japan, Volume Five: The Nineteenth Century*, edited by Marius Jansen, 367–431. Cambridge: Cambridge University Press, 1989.

Wigen, Kären. *The Making of a Japanese Periphery, 1750–1920*. Berkeley: University of California Press, 1995.

Wray, William D. *Mitsubishi and the N.Y.K., 1870–1914: Business Strategy in the Japanese Shipping Industry*. Cambridge, MA: Harvard University Press, 1984.

Yamamoto Kakuma. *Yamamoto Kakuma kenpakusho* Dōshisha Daigaku Gakujutsu Jōhō Senta Dōshisha Shiryōshitsu, 1869 [cited March 5, 2005. Available from http://duels.doshisha.ac.jp:88/denshika/yamamoto/128/imgidx128.html.

Yamamura, Kozo. "The Meiji Land Tax Reform and its Effects." In *Japan in Transition: From Tokugawa to Meiji*, edited by Marius Jansen and Gilbert Rozman, 382–99. Princeton, NJ: Princeton University Press, 1986.

Yao, Xinzhong. *An Introduction to Confucianism*. Cambridge: Cambridge University Press, 2000.

Yokoi Shōnan. "Kokuze sanron." In *Nihon no meichō 30- Sakuma Shōzan, Yokoi Shōnan*, edited by Matsuura Ryō, 309–35. Tokyo: Chūō Kōronsha, 1970.

Yoshikawa Hidezo. "Maeda Masana no shokusan kōgyō undō." *Dōshisha shōgaku* 14, nos. 3–4 (1962): 54–80.

Yūri Kimimasa. "Kinsatsu hakkō ni kansuru dajōkan fukoku." In *Keizai kōsō*, edited by Nakamura Masanori and Ishii Kanji, 5–6. Tokyo: Iwanami Shoten, 1988.

Zhu Xi. "Preface to the *Great Learning* by Chapter and Phrase." In *Sources of Chinese Tradition*, edited by Wm. Theodore DeBary and Irene Bloom, 721–25. New York: Columbia University Press, 1999.

Index